Quick and Easy
CAKE TOPPERS

Quick and Easy
CAKE TOPPERS

100 Little Sugar Decorations to Make

Search Press

First published in 2020

Search Press Limited
Wellwood, North Farm Road,
Tunbridge Wells, Kent TN2 3DR

Previously published in 2016 as *100 Little Sugar Decorations to Make* using material from the following books in the *Twenty to Make* series published by Search Press:

Sugar Animals by Frances McNaughton, 2009
Sugar Fairies by Frances McNaughton, 2010
Sugar Flowers by Lisa Slatter, 2011
Sugar Birds by Frances McNaughton, 2011
Mini Sugar Shoes by Frances McNaughton, 2012
Sugar Sporties by Paula MacLeod, 2012
Sugar Wobblies by Georgie Godbold, 2013
Mini Sugar Bags by Frances McNaughton, 2013
Sugar Scaries by Frances McNaughton, 2013
Sugar Dogs by Frances McNaughton, 2014
Sugar Christmas Decorations by Georgie Godbold, 2014
Sugar Brides & Grooms by Katrien van Zyl, 2015

Text copyright © Frances McNaughton, Georgie Godbold, Katrien van Zyl, Lisa Slatter and Paula MacLeod 2016

Photographs by Paul Bricknell, Debbie Patterson, Johan van Zyl and Vanessa Davies

Photographs and design copyright
© Search Press Ltd 2016

ISBN: 978-1-78221-804-3

Suppliers
If you have difficulty in obtaining any of the materials and equipment mentioned in this book, then please visit the Search Press website for details of suppliers:
www.searchpress.com

CONTENTS

Labrador Puppy,
page 22

Snowflake Fairy, page 24

Panda, page 26

Blushing Bride, page 28

Purple Banana Bag,
page 32

Frog, page 34

Daisy, page 36

Rose Fairy, page 38

Puffin, page 40

Dracula, page 42

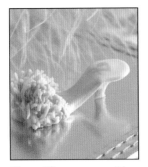

Kitten Slipper, page 44

Football, page 46

Dachshund, page 50

Penguin, page 52

Hippopotamus, page 54

Handsome Groom, page 56

Red Glitter Bag, page 60

Sheep, page 62

Viola, page 66

Blossom Fairy, page 68

Owl, page 70

Gruesome Gargoyle, page 72

Strappy Sandal, page 74

Beach Volleyball,
page 76

Schnauzer, page 78

Snowman, page 80

Dolphin, page 82

Sweet Bride, page 84

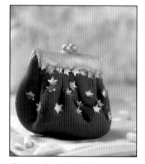

Starry Evening Bag,
page 86

Zebra, page 88

Hydrangea, page 90

Daisy Fairy, page 92

Mallard, page 94

Cake Kraken, page 96

Flip Flops, page 98

Running, page 100

Scottie Dog, page 102

Christmas Elf, page 104

Tiger, page 108

Dancing Groom, page 110

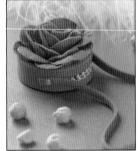

Pink Rose Bag, page 112

Chick, page 114

Gerbera, page 116

Dancing Fairy, page 118

Robin, page 120

Mean Merlin, page 122

Baby Sneakers, page 124

Windsurfing, page 126

Yorkshire Terrier, page 128

Mouse, page 130

Seal, page 132

Ruby Bride, page 134

Zebra Print Bag, page 136

Dinosaur, page 138

Freesia, page 140

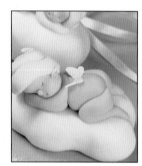

Baby Fairy, page 142

Penguin, page 144

Vampire Bat, page 146

Football Boots, page 148

Sailing, page 150

Bichon Frise, page 154

Reindeer, page 156

Koala Bear, page 158

Romantic Groom, page 160

Gel Bag, page 162

Piggy, page 164

Carnation, page 166

Christmas Fairy, page 168

Green Woodpecker, page 170

Frankie Stein, page 172

Elf Boots, page 174

Skiing, page 176

Bassett Hound, page 180

Angel, page 182

Lion, page 186

Country Bride, page 188

Denim Bag, page 190

Elephant, page 192

Rose, page 194

Fairy Godmother,
page 196

Cockatoo, page 198

Evil Clown, page 200

Patriotic Platforms,
page 202

Dalmatian, page 204

Father Christmas,
page 206

Crocodile, page 210

Indian Groom, page 212

Designer Satchel,
page 214

Ladybird, page 216

Lily, page 218

Cupcake Fairy, page 220

Rooster, page 222

Wicked Witch, page 224

Leopard Shoe, page 226

Sheepdog, page 228

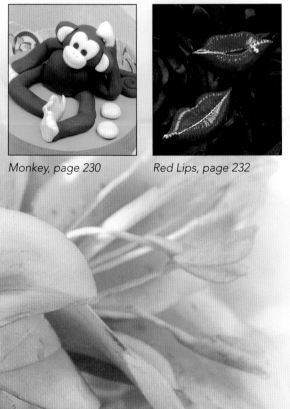

Monkey, page 230

Red Lips, page 232

Hummingbird, page 234

Arachnophobia,
page 236

Men's Slippers, page 238

INTRODUCTION

If you love sugarcraft, is the book for you. This fabulous book is absolutely packed full of diverse sugarcraft projects that will delight and inspire beginner and seasoned sugarcrafters alike. Designed by five talented and experienced authors, these lovely projects are the work of Frances McNaughton, Georgie Godbold, Katrien van Zyl, Lisa Slatter and Paula McLeod.

The range of projects includes sugar animals, flowers, shoes, birds, fairies, sporty characters, wobbly characters, brides and grooms, scary characters, mini bags, tiny dogs and Christmas decorations, so there is something here for everyone to choose from. There are useful lists of materials and tools at the beginning, which explain what you need to make these charming projects. You can use these little

sugar decorations as wonderful cake toppers or simply as decorations in their own right – the choice is yours. They also make lovely, personalised gifts for family and friends.

Projects include a hippo, a skier, a ruby bride, a wicked witch, a red glitter bag, a reindeer, a gerbera, a rose fairy, a Scottie dog, a puffin, a sheep and a strappy sandal. Whatever the occasion, there is a wealth of inspiration here with projects for all skill levels that will make the perfect centrepiece for birthdays, christenings, anniversaries, weddings, Valentine's Day, Halloween and Christmas.

Happy sugarcrafting!

MATERIALS

The main materials you will need to make all the sugar decorations in this book are:

Modelling paste Some of the models use modelling paste – fondant (sugarpaste) strengthened with CMC (cellulose gum) or gum tragacanth. Use 250g/8oz fondant (sugarpaste) to approximately half a teaspoon of the gum. This is used when parts need to dry harder, for example, long beaks and parts that need to stand. Leave for a few hours for the gum to develop before using.

Fondant (sugarpaste) This paste is commercially available as coloured fondant (sugarpaste). White fondant (sugarpaste) can also be coloured with strong edible food colours from sugarcraft shops and some supermarkets. It is not advisable to use liquid colours when making dark or bold colours, as this makes the fondant sticky and unworkable.

Mexican paste is also known as flower paste or gum paste (see page 21). It is used to make anything that needs to dry quickly and hold its shape, such as flowers.

Sugar glue is made by slowly warming 15g (½oz) of fondant and 15ml (½fl oz) of water in the microwave until it boils. When cool, it is ready for use. Sugar glue keeps well in a small screw-top jar.

Strong gel paste colours are used for mixing in to white modelling paste to make solid colours.

Icing sugar and **cornstarch (cornflour)** can both be used when rolling out paste to stop it sticking. Use it sparingly as they will dry paste out too much if you are not careful.

White fat stops the paste sticking to the board if it is too dry when rolling out.

Other materials you will need are:

Chenille sticks, also called pipe cleaners, can be obtained in various colours from craft shops.

Clear piping gel is used to to glue and gloss.

Confectioner's glaze will allow you to give a shiny finish to painted noses.

Edible candy sticks These can be either bought or made and dried in advance. Mix 250g (9oz) of fondant (sugarpaste) or royal icing with half a teaspoon of tylose powder, CMC or gum tragacanth. Roll into thin sausages, cut to short lengths and allow to dry for at least 24 hours or longer.

Edible food colour powder Available in plain and pearl colours, brushed onto the surface to add soft colour or an iridescent sheen.

Edible food colouring pens are useful for drawing on features.

Edible metallic paint gold and silver can be used to great effect.

Edible sprinkles are used for decoration.

Edible wafer paper This can be used to make birds' wings and other delicate components.

Food grade alcohol This is used mixed with edible powder food colour, for painting.

Edible glitter Use only glitter labelled 'For food contact', and remember to remind people if the figures you make are non-edible.

Styrofoam (polystyrene) balls can be found in most craft shops or art shops.

Leaf gelatine sheets These can be used in conjunction with modelling paste to form transparent areas.

Royal icing is used to pipe hair on to figures, and as an adhesive.

Small black edible sugar pearls These make good eyes and noses.

Vegetable cooking oil To stop the paste sticking to your hands and tools, rub a small amount of this into your hands and your work surface.

Joining fondant (sugarpaste) shapes

Most parts can be stuck together just by dampening them with water. Make sure that the paste is only dampened – do not wet the surface too much, or the pieces will just slide off. Fresh egg white can also be used as a slightly stickier glue. You can also use thick edible glue. This is useful for attaching dried sugar pieces (for instance, wings and heads) and for when a stronger glue is needed. Mix a pinch of modelling paste with a few drops of water by mashing it with a palette knife until it forms a stringy, sticky glue, also called gunge. If you make this glue with the same colour paste that you used on the model, it will be easier to conceal.

Useful materials
Items such as edible candy sticks, piping gel, edible powder food colours and edible sugar pearls are widely used in sugarcrafting.

TOOLS

You will need these basic tools for nearly all the projects in this book. They can all be obtained from sugarcraft shops or online cake decorating suppliers:

A pointed tool, a **smiley tool** or **drinking straw**, **paintbrushes** for dusting paste or attaching pieces together, a **texture frilling tool**, and a **ball tool**, a **dogbone tool** and a **Dresden tool**. Note that some of the tools are double-ended – the pointed tool has one pointed and one rounded end, for example.

A non-stick work board makes it easier to roll out the paste without it moving. Place a **non-slip mat** underneath to prevent your board from moving.

Small non-stick rolling pin This is used for rolling out your paste. There are many different sizes and patterns of **textured rolling pins**. They can be obtained from cake decorating suppliers or online.

Small pair of scissors These are used to cut paste or ribbons.

Use a small thin **palette knife** to release paste from your board.

Cutters, made of plastic or metal, come in various shapes such as ovals, circles or hearts. Small **blossom cutters** are easy-to-use flower-shaped cutters that come in many sizes. A **Garrett frill cutter** can make large circle frills.

Cocktail sticks are used to support the bodies and for texturing.

Craft knife A sharp blade is essential in order to ensure safe cutting.

Mini digital scales are ideal for weighing out small amounts of paste.

Multi-mould This can be used to make a tiny crown, wings, bow, a tiny flower, a tiny faceted star and many other small items.

Small pieces of **foam** help support sugar items whilst they are drying.

A stamen is a round bead attached to a stick. These can be used when making flowers or for eyes.

Icing tubes are used to make circles, buttons or dots.

Small wire cutters are used to cut cocktail sticks, chenille sticks or wires to the required length.

To make very thin strands of fondant (sugarpaste) for hair or fluff, use a **clay gun, tea strainer** or **sieve** to push the fondant (sugarpaste) through the mesh.

You will also need some more specific tools for making some of the decorations:

Butterfly wings can be made in flower/gum paste using a cutter, or bought ready made from card.

Bell moulds come in many different sizes and can be obtained from sugarcraft shops or online cake decorating suppliers.

Other cutters you may need are: an **eight-petal flower cutter**, a **carnation cutter**, a **calyx (five-point) cutter**, a variety of **butterfly cutters**, an **oak leaf cutter**, and a **daisy cutter**.

Bulbous cone tool Push this into the centre of a flower to open up the centre.

Cake dummy You can push wired flowers into this to dry.

Cutting wheel This is used for cutting shapes from rolled fondant (sugarpaste).

Design wheel For adding large stitch and zigzag patterns and lines.

Dowel When making mini shoes, shoe soles are laid over a pen or pencil, acting as a dowel to create the high-heeled shape.

Dusting brush This is used for applying edible powder food colour, or edible glitter.

Flower and leaf cutters These are available in a vast array of shapes and sizes, in metal or plastic.

Food colour felt-tip pen This is for making edible marks such as eyes.

Food-grade kebab, barbecue or **cake-pop sticks**.

Kitchen paper This is used when dusting and drying flowers and leaves.

Leaf veiners These are an integral part of plunger cutters; just cut out the leaf shape, then push the plunger down on to the surface to vein the front of the leaf. They are also available separately, in which case they are usually double-sided and made from food-grade silicone. The leaf is placed inside and the veiners are squashed together to create a veined surface on the front and back of the leaf.

Lustre spray Pearl, gold, bronze, pink – this is spray food colour with sparkle.

Mexican foam balling pad Use this when softening, cupping and shaping the edges of petals. It is not essential as you could use the palm of your hand instead, but these pads are ideal for people with hot hands.

Music stave cutter Useful for cutting thin strips of modelling paste or fondant (sugarpaste).

Petal veining tool This is used to create a fluted or frilled edge. The scoop end is great for sprinkling glitter.

Piping bag and tubes These are used for piping leaves, stems, petals and other parts.

Plastic food bag/airtight box For keeping paste soft.

Ribbon Use this to back flower sprays and fill in gaps.

Small drinking straw This should be cut off at an angle, and is used for making mouths and closed eyes.

Small long-nosed pliers Bending wires in place is much easier and safer with this tool.

Small plain piping tubes These are for cutting tiny circles for eyes etc.

Stem tape This is a stretchy self-sticking paper tape used to cover wires for flower making. Attach stamens to the ends of wires and to bind flowers together into sprays, posies and arrangements. It can also be used to make stamens.

Stitching wheel This is used to add a stitched effect.

Tape cutter This cuts stem tape down into thinner widths for ease of use.

Tapered and serrated cone tools Push these into the centre of a flower to mark a star shape or marking guidelines.

Tweezers Useful for picking up tiny pieces of paste.

White alcohol Mix this with food colours for painting. Alcohol evaporates quickly, ensuring no surface damage is done to the icing. You can use dipping solution, rejuvenator spirit, lemon extract or clear vanilla essence instead.

Wires Paper-covered wire is good, the thickness of which is measured in gauge (g), 18g being the thickest and 33g being the thinnest. Choose a gauge of wire to suit the weight and size of your flower.

BEFORE YOU START

Basic shapes

Several of the models in this book use the same basic body and head shapes. Follow the instructions on this page to make them. Individual projects will indicate when this type of basic body or head should be used.

Basic bodies

1 Roll 45g (1½oz) of modelling paste into a ball.

2 Shape the paste into a cone 6.5cm (2½in) tall.

3 Insert an 8cm (3⅛in) cocktail stick through the middle of the cone to the base for support. The top of the cocktail stick will support the head. Make two holes in the front for the legs to fit in.

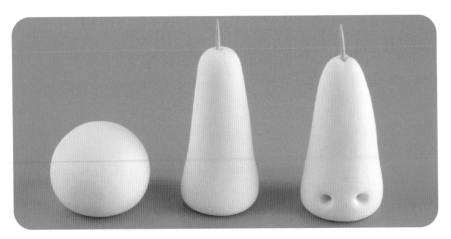

Heads

1 Roll 20g (⅔oz) of modelling paste into a smooth ball. Make a small hole in the middle of the face ready for the nose.

2 Make a small round-ended cone of paste for the nose and insert it into the hole using a small amount of sugar glue.

3 Use a smiley tool or drinking straw to make the mouth.

4 Make two holes for the eyes and leave to dry.

Eyes

1 These are made using stamens (see below). Insert them into the head and leave to dry. If you cannot obtain stamens, you can use two very small balls of white paste for the eyes.

2 Use a fine black fibre-tip pen to mark the pupils onto the stamens or paste.

Modelling paste recipe (for 250g/9oz)

If you want to make your own modelling paste, simply follow this recipe:

1 Break 250g (9oz) of fondant (sugarpaste) into small pieces. Sprinkle 2.5–5ml (½–1tsp) CMC, gum tragacanth or Tylose edible gum powder over the fondant (sugarpaste), depending on how stiff you want it; the more powder, the firmer the paste.

2 Spread white vegetable fat (shortening) on your hands and knead the gum into the paste. Knead in food colouring if the paste was not coloured before.

3 Cover with plastic wrap and leave to rest for a few hours or overnight. Always knead well before working with it and rolling it out. Add white vegetable fat if it feels dry. Roll out on a cutting mat using a non-stick roller.

Mexican paste recipe

Mexican paste, also known as flower/gum paste, is a sugar modelling paste made with gum, which makes it stronger and allows it to be rolled out thinly. It dries slowly, going leathery before it dries hard. It is available commercially or can be made using the following recipe:

1 Place 225g (8oz) icing sugar into a bowl. Add three 5ml teaspoons of gum tragacanth. Mix the dry ingredients together. Add six 5ml teaspoons of cold water. Stir by hand until it becomes crumbly but damp enough to bind together. Add a little more water if too dry, or icing sugar if too wet. Turn out on to a worktop and knead until pliable. Place in a plastic food bag and leave at room temperature for 12 hours until firm.

2 Break off a small piece and knead between your palms. Continue kneading between your fingers. Repeat until all the paste is softened. The paste can be used immediately.

3 Store paste in an airtight container at room temperature, never in the fridge. If you have leftover paste, wrap each piece in plastic wrap and place all of the pieces into a plastic food bag and place them in the freezer. Defrost only the quantity required for using. Smaller pieces will defrost more quickly.

Note: Mexican (flower/gum) paste can also be coloured by adding strong paste food colours. When making dark colours, the paste can become very soft, so it can be better to use ready-coloured black, red and purple paste.

LABRADOR PUPPY

Materials:

- 25g (just under 1oz) cream-coloured modelling paste
- Edible candy stick
- Edible black sugar pearls
- Dark brown edible powder food colour

Tools:

- Small petal cutter
- Dresden tool
- Dusting brush
- Water brush
- Small, non-stick rolling pin
- Thin palette knife

Instructions:

1 Shape 10g (⅓oz) of modelling paste to a 3cm (1¼in) oval for the body. Insert a candy stick right through, as a support. Cut the stick to form a short neck. Pinch and shape a small pointed tail. Stand the body up.

2 Cut 6g (⅕oz) of modelling paste into four equal pieces for the legs. Roll each leg to about 3cm (1¼in). For the back legs, flatten the top end. Mark toes with the palette knife. Attach the legs to the body by dampening with a little water.

3 For the head, make a 5g (⅙oz) ball of modelling paste. Roll one end with your fingers to form the muzzle. Mark the eyes and nose with a Dresden tool. Push the black sugar pearls in for the eyes and nose.

4 Dampen the candy stick neck, and gently push the head into place on the body.

5 Make two very tiny sausages of paste and attach over the eyes.

6 Roll out a small amount of paste thinly and cut out two ears using the small petal cutter as shown. Mark the surface with the Dresden tool, then brush the surface gently with dark brown powder food colour. Dampen the underneath surface of the ears with the water brush and attach the ears at the back of the head, folding them forwards towards the face.

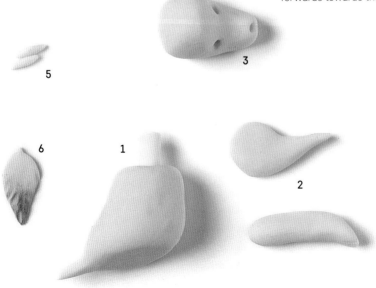

5

3

6

1

2

Liz
Pretty and pink, with lots of glitter, everyone will love the Snowflake Fairy! The small snowflakes can be fragile, so make one or two spare in case of accidents.

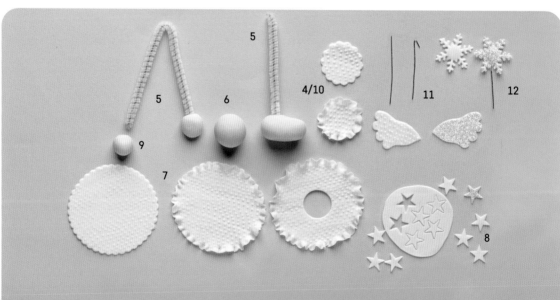

5

5

6

4/10

11

12

9

7

8

SNOWFLAKE FAIRY

Materials:

- 60g (2⅛oz) pale pink modelling paste
- 25g (⅝oz) flesh-coloured modelling paste
- Small amount of Mexican (flower/gum) paste in white
- Pale pink royal icing
- Pale pink dusting powder

One white chenille stick

White glitter

Cocktail stick

Two 4cm (1½in) lengths of wire

Tools:

Cutters: small star, snowflake, butterfly wings

Blossom cutters: 7cm (2¾in) and 3cm (1³⁄₁₆in)

Textured rolling pin with dots

No. 2 icing nozzle and piping bag

Sugar glue

Small pieces of foam

Fine black fibre-tip pen

Instructions:

1 Make a basic body in pink as shown on page 20.

2 Roll 20g (⅔oz) of flesh-coloured paste into a smooth ball for the head. Use a pointed tool to make a hole for the nose, and the smiley tool to mark the mouth.

3 Roll a small ball of flesh-coloured paste into a cone for the nose, then use a little glue to secure the pointed end into the hole in the head. When the head is completely dry, draw on the eyes using a fine black fibre-tip pen. Dust the cheeks with pink dusting powder.

4 Make two leg frills by rolling out the white paste and cutting out two 3cm (1³⁄₁₆in) blossoms. Frill the edges of both pieces with the rounded end of the pointed tool, then use a little sugar glue to secure them over the leg holes. Use the pointed tool to remake the holes.

5 Cut a chenille stick into two 7.5cm (3in) lengths for the legs and one 12cm (4¾in) length for the arms.

6 Roll 12g (5/12oz) of pink paste into a ball and cut it in half to make two oval shoes. Lightly glue one end of a 7.5cm (3in) chenille stick and insert it into a shoe. Lightly glue the shoe and cover with white glitter, then shake off the excess. Add glue to the other end of the chenille stick and insert it into the body. Repeat with the other leg and shoe. Leave to dry.

7 Roll out a circle of white paste with the patterned rolling pin. Use the 7cm (2¾in) blossom cutter to cut out one skirt. Frill the outer edge with the rounded end of the pointed tool. Use the large end of an icing nozzle to cut out a hole in the middle. Add glue to the body just above the leg frills. Pull the skirt down over the cocktail stick and secure in place. Support with foam.

8 Decorate the waist with small stars cut out from the remaining white paste, attaching them with glue.

9 Roll 3g (⅛oz) of flesh-coloured paste into a ball and cut in half to make two oval hands. Add a little sugar glue to each end of the 12cm (4¾in) chenille stick and attach the hands. Bend the chenille stick around the back of the cocktail stick and glue it in place, bringing the arms and hands down. Shape into position when dry.

10 Roll out a circle of white paste with the patterned rolling pin. Cut two 3cm (1³⁄₁₆in) blossoms for neck frills. Soften the edges with the rounded end of the pointed tool. Add glue to the cocktail stick and place the frills on individually. Press down firmly at the front and back over the chenille stick, before gluing the head on firmly. Pipe the hair as shown, using a small amount of royal icing.

11 Use the wing cutter and the white paste to cut out a pair of wings. Leave to dry, then attach to the back of the body using a little royal icing. Support with foam if necessary until dry.

12 Roll out some white Mexican paste and cut out five snowflakes. Glue one to the bottom of each shoe and one on the hands. Place a small length of wire on to the back of a snowflake with a little glue. Press on a very small ball of white paste. Repeat with the other snowflake. When dry, add glue and apply glitter. Push into the top of the head through the royal icing. Leave to dry.

The baby panda is just a smaller
version of its mum, lying in a more
relaxed position. It has a pink nose
to make it extra cute.

PANDA

Materials:

35g (1¼oz) white
   fondant (sugarpaste)

30g (1oz) black
   fondant (sugarpaste)

Tiny piece of pink
   fondant (sugarpaste)

Candy stick

Tools:

Cocktail stick

Drinking straw

Sharp pointed scissors

Thin palette knife

Heart cutter, 2.5cm (1in)

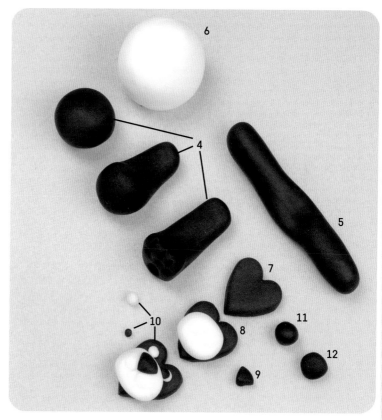

Instructions:

1 Divide the white paste into about 25g (just under 1oz) for the body, 10g (⅓oz) for the head and a pea-sized piece for the cheeks and eyes.

2 Make the body into an egg shape with a candy stick for support (not shown).

3 Divide the black paste into four balls: two for the legs, one for the arms and one for the face, nose, ears, eyes and tail.

4 For the legs, form two of the black balls into pear shapes. Shape a foot at the fat end. Mark claws with a cocktail stick. Attach the narrow end of each leg to the body.

5 For the arms, make one long sausage from the other black ball. Stick on top of the body.

6 Make the head from a ball of white paste, approximately half the size of the body.

7 Cut out a black heart shape for the face, using the heart cutter.

8 Attach an oval of white on to the heart shape. Mark two curves, side by side, for the mouth, using a drinking straw.

9 Make a black triangle for the nose.

10 For the eyes, press two tiny balls of white and then two even smaller balls of black on to the heart shape. Stick the face on to the head. Attach the head to the top of the body.

11 For the ears, make two small balls of black paste and shape them to make indents.

12 Make the tail from a small ball of black paste.

13 Stick on three small pink balls to each foot for the toe pads, and a larger one for the sole of the foot.

BLUSHING BRIDE

Materials:

Modelling paste: flesh-coloured: 13g (½oz);
   black: pinhead-sized piece; brown: 5g (⅙oz); white: 63g
   (2¹⁄₁₀oz); red: 3g (¹⁄₁₀oz)

Sugar/spaghetti sticks

Edible glue/pasteurised egg white

White and black gel food colouring

Pink dusting powder

Tools:

Cutting mat

Non-stick rolling pin

Scalpel/craft knife

Small paintbrush

Piping nozzle (tube)

Toothpick

Dresden tool/skewer

1

12

9

13

7

10

8

Instructions:

1 To make the head and face, first pinch off a tiny piece of paste from 10g (⅓oz) of flesh-coloured paste to use for a nose and two cone-shaped ears. Roll the rest of the paste into a 2.5cm (1in) ball/cone. Indent the ball/cone horizontally in the centre front by rubbing your finger over it, pushing slightly into the paste.

2 Use the widest end of the piping nozzle to make an indentation for a mouth. Pull the nozzle slightly downwards when pulling it away to make a lower lip.

3 Attach the nose and ears with a tiny drop of edible glue or egg white. Flatten each ear with a Dresden or ball tool.

4 Roll two pinhead-sized balls of black paste for the eyes and flatten them with your finger, or roll out a pea-sized piece of black paste on your cutting mat and cut out two circles with the narrow end of a no. 3 piping nozzle. Attach the eyes to the face with a tiny drop of edible glue or egg white. Dip the tip of a toothpick into white gel food colouring and dab a dot on the right side of each eye.

5 Dust pink dusting powder on the cheeks with your finger. Dip the tip of a small paintbrush into black or brown gel food colouring and swipe it at the top of each eye to make one or two long eyelashes. Paint thin eyebrows above each eye.

6 Make a hole in the bottom of the head with a toothpick and let it dry for a few hours or overnight.

7 For the dress, roll 60g (2oz) of white paste into a large, thin cone 8.5cm (3½in) long. Place the cone upright and indent the top with a Dresden tool/skewer. Push a long sugar stick or a few pieces of uncooked spaghetti through the cone all the way to the bottom of the dress and protruding 1.5cm (⅔in) above the dress.

8 For the shoes, roll 3g (⅒oz) of white paste into two ovals and attach them to the bottom of the dress with edible glue.

9 Make the neck by rolling a pea-sized piece of flesh-coloured paste into a tapered sausage. Place it onto the protruding sugar stick/spaghetti to make a neck.

10 To make the arms roll 3g (⅒oz) of flesh-coloured paste into two sausages, each 4.5cm (1¾in) long. Roll the end of each sausage between your index fingers to make a wrist and flatten the end of each arm to form a hand. Bend each arm in the middle and attach to the sides of the body with a drop of edible glue/egg white.

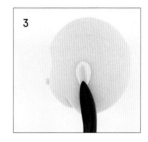

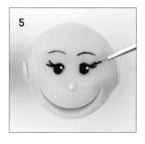

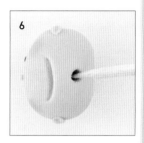

11 Place the dried head on the neck, attaching it with a drop of edible glue and leave to dry for a few hours or overnight before attaching the hair.

12 Make the hair by rolling long and short tapered sausages from the brown paste. Glue a few short tapered sausages to the back of the head to cover the neck. Glue long, tapered straight sausages to the head, starting on top at the back of the head. Make a parting in front by gluing hair from the centre or from one side of the head to the sides of the face..

13 Make the bouquet of roses. Roll out the red paste until almost paper thin. Cut it into thin strips with a scalpel/craft knife. Roll up the strips to form tiny roses. Attach to the hands with edible glue.

PURPLE BANANA BAG

Materials:

Mexican (flower/gum) paste in
purple

Tools:

Small, non-stick rolling pin

6cm (2⅜in) and 2.5cm (1in)
circle cutters

2cm (¾in) and 1cm (⅜in) oval
cutters

Fine stitching wheel

Instructions:

1 Roll out the paste thinly. Cut out two 6cm (2⅜in) circles, two 2cm (¾in)
ovals and one 1cm (⅜in) oval.

2 Shape a large pea-sized piece of paste into a 6cm (2⅜in) banana shape.
Attach it just inside the edge of one of the 6cm (2⅜in) circles. Dampen the edge
of the circle and stick it to the banana part.

3 Attach the second circle on top of the first one, curving and smoothing the
edge over the bottom to hide the join. Use the 2.5cm (1in) circle cutter to cut
the hole for the handle.

4 Mark the bag with the stitching wheel as shown.

5 For the bow, fold the two 2cm (¾in) ovals in half and pinch the narrow ends.
Dampen and press the ends together and lay the 1cm (⅜in) oval across the join,
tucking the ends under.

6 Dampen the bow and attach it to the bag.

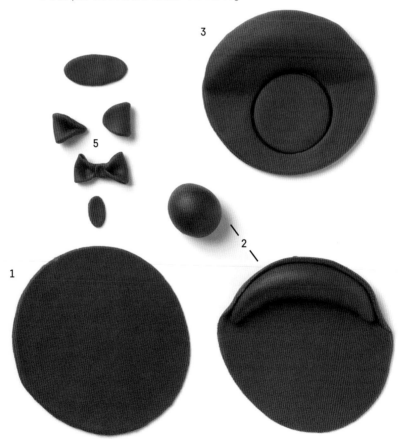

Dave
The tiny frog is just a smaller version of his dad, sitting in a watering can and waiting to jump out.

FROG

Instructions:

1 Make a basic body in green (see page 20) but do not make any holes in the front.

2 Roll 20g (⅔oz) of green paste into a smooth ball for the head, flatten it into an thin oval and mark it as shown using a cocktail stick.

3 Cut 4g (⅛oz) of green paste in half and roll each part into a smooth ball. With the round end of a pointed tool, make a large hole, insert a small ball of white paste then insert a small ball of black paste in the corner for the pupil. Repeat to make two eyes.

4 Cut 16g (½oz) of green paste into four. Shape each one into a flat oval disc and mark with a palette knife as shown to make the pads.

5 To make the ankles, cut 10g (⅓oz) of green paste into four and roll each one into a smooth round ball. With a little sugar glue, attach one on the top of each pad, then use a pointed tool to make a small hole on the top of each one.

6 For the arms, bend a 16cm (6¼in) green chenille stick in half, add a little sugar glue to the ends and attach a pad to each. Bend the chenille stick around the back of the cocktail stick, then glue it in place, bringing the pads down in front of the body.

7 Cut two 11cm (4⅜in) lengths of chenille stick and shape as shown for the legs. Glue each end and attach a pad to one. Insert the other end into the base of the body at the back. Repeat with the other leg and pad.

8 Secure the head on to the cocktail stick using a little sugar glue while pressing down firmly. Attach the eyes on top of the head using a little sugar glue.

Materials:

100g (3½oz) lime green modelling paste

Small amounts of magenta, yellow and black modelling paste

Two stripy green chenille sticks

Cocktail stick

Paintbrushes

Texture frilling tool

Ball tool

Small, non-stick rolling pin

Small pair of scissors

Small thin palette knife

Sugar glue

Tools:

Pointed tool

Smiley tool/drinking straw

9 Roll out a small amount of yellow paste, shape it into a small crown and use sugar glue to attach it in place behind the eyes. Make three small balls of yellow paste for the top of the crown and glue them on.

10 Roll out the magenta paste and tie it into a bow, then use sugar glue to attach it at the top of the body.

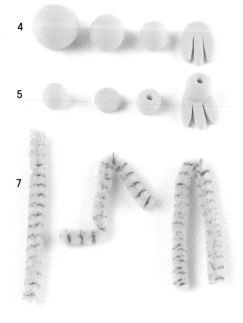

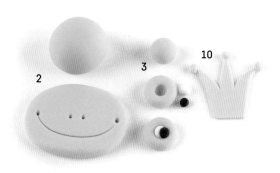

35

Peach Daisy
For an alternative look (left) try dusting the edges of the petals with peach powdered food colour.

A   B   C   D   E

F   G   H   I   J

K   L   M

DAISY

Materials:

Mexican (flower/gum) paste in white, green and yellow

Powdered food colour in pink

Royal icing: white

Tools:

Daisy marguerite plunger cutters: 35mm (1⅜in) and 20mm (¾in)

Daisy leaf cutter

Creative plaque embossing cutter: 75mm (3in)

Sieve

Mexican foam modelling pad

Dresden tool

Paintbrush: 12mm (½in) flat

Pearl lustre spray with spray gun attachment

Instructions:

Flowers

1 On a non-stick surface, roll out some white Mexican paste quite thinly. Cut out a daisy shape using the largest cutter (A).

2 Use a craft knife or mini cutting wheel to make a central cut along each petal to divide it into two (B).

3 Lay a mini modelling tool vertically down the centre of one petal, with the tip of the tool at the centre of the flower, then roll from side to side to widen and thin the petal. Ensure you use cornflour on your board and tool to stop the paste from sticking (C).

4 Continue to roll each petal in turn until you have completed the whole flower (D).

5 Prepare another large daisy shape in the same way as above, then paint a little sugar glue on to the centre of one of the large daisy shapes and stick the other on top (E).

6 Cut out a small daisy shape and divide each of the petals in half (F).

7 Roll each petal from side to side to widen and thin (G).

8 Roll a pea-sized ball of yellow Mexican paste (H) then push the ball against the surface of a sieve to flatten into a textured disc (I).

9 Paint the centre of the small prepared daisy shape with sugar glue and stick the yellow textured disc into the centre. Wrap the petals up around the sides of the disc, using a little sugar glue to secure if necessary (J).

10 Stick the centre into the middle of the layered larger petals (K).

Leaves

11 From green Mexican paste, cut out two daisy leaves, pull a vein down the centre and several more from the central vein out to the outer edge using a Dresden tool (L).

12 Place on a Mexican foam modelling pad and soften the edges by rubbing a ball or bone tool all around the edges (M).

13 Once dry, use the flat brush to dust the edges of the petal with a little pink powdered food colour, spray the leaves with pearl lustre colour and arrange flower and leaves on a plaque with a little royal icing (see left).

Go Green!
As an alternative, you can use green liquorice sticks for the arms and legs and white fondant (sugarpaste) for the rest of the fairy. These two make a beautiful, petal-covered pair.

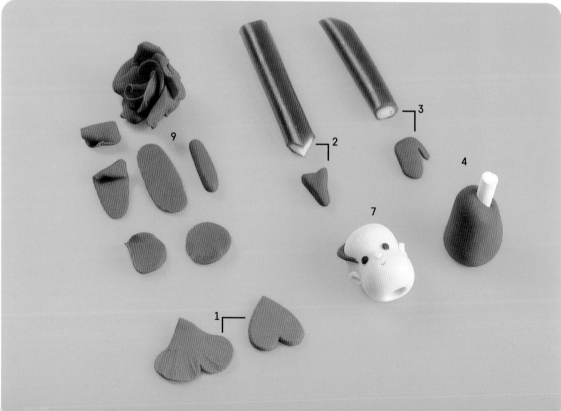

ROSE FAIRY

Materials:

10g (⅓oz) flesh-coloured fondant (sugarpaste) for the head

Red fondant (sugarpaste): 10g (⅓oz) for the body and
10g (⅓oz) for the hands, shoes and hair

10g (⅓oz) red modelling paste for the wings, rose petal
skirt and rose hat

Candy stick

Four strawberry liquorice sticks

Tiny amount of black fondant (sugarpaste) for the eyes

Tools:

27mm (1⅛in) heart cutter

Small drinking straw

Non-stick rolling pin

Thin palette knife

Plastic sandwich bag

Water brush

Dresden tool or cocktail stick

Tissue paper

Instructions:

1 For the wings, roll out the red modelling paste and cut out two hearts with the heart cutter. Roll a cocktail stick over the rounded edges to frill them slightly. Leave to dry for a few hours or overnight.

2 For the legs, cut two strawberry liquorice sticks to 6.5cm (2½in), and cut them to a point for the feet. For the shoes, shape two pea-sized pieces of red fondant (sugarpaste) to a point. Dampen the pointed ends of the legs and attach the shoes.

3 For the arms, cut two strawberry liquorice sticks to 5cm (2in), and cut them to an angle for the shoulder ends. For the hands, make two pea-sized pieces of red fondant (sugarpaste) to form simple hand shapes, cut out a tiny triangle from each to form thumbs. Dampen the flat ends of the arms and attach the hands.

4 Make an egg shape of the red fondant (sugarpaste) for the body with a candy stick for support, slightly sticking out. Dampen the top ends of the legs and push into the body.

5 Make red petals for the skirt using pea-sized pieces of fondant (sugarpaste), flattened and thinned at the edge by pressing them in a plastic sandwich bag. Attach the petals around the body.

6 Dampen the top of the arms and push into the body.

7 For the head, pinch off a piece of the flesh-coloured fondant (sugarpaste). Use this to make two tiny teardrop shapes for the ears and a tiny pin-head piece for the nose.

Form the rest into a ball and use a finger to roll a slight indentation across the middle. Make a hole in the neck end using a dry candy stick. Attach the nose in the centre of the face, and press a mouth shape with the cut drinking straw under the nose. Dampen the sides of the head in line with the nose. Stick the ears on and press in place using a Dresden tool or cocktail stick, forming the ear shape. Make two tiny pin-head size pieces of black fondant (sugarpaste) for the eyes. Dampen the face to stick them on, slightly above the nose.

8 For the hair, make lots of small carrot-shaped pieces using red fondant (sugarpaste). Dampen the head and attach hair strands with the pointed end towards the face. When the head is covered with enough strands of hair, cut out some tiny blossoms in different colours and stick on to the top of the head. Dampen the end of the candy stick neck, and attach the head.

9 To make the rose hat, form one pea-sized piece of red modelling paste to a small sausage shape. Flatten along one edge and roll it up along the thicker edge to form a spiral. Make nine more pea-sized pieces of red modelling paste. Flatten them by pressing around the edge in a plastic sandwich bag. Attach three petals, overlapping and dampening. Stick on another two or three petals, then attach them to the top of the head, finishing off with the remaining petals. Make more petals if necessary.

10 Attach the wings with thick edible glue/gunge. Support with scrunched-up tissue paper until dry.

Who could resist making this cute clown of the bird world?

PUFFIN

Materials:

- 25g (just under 1oz) black fondant (sugarpaste)
- Small pieces of white, orange, red, yellow and blue fondant (sugarpaste)

Tools:

- Heart cutter: 2.5cm (1in)
- Small rolling pin
- Dresden tool/cocktail stick

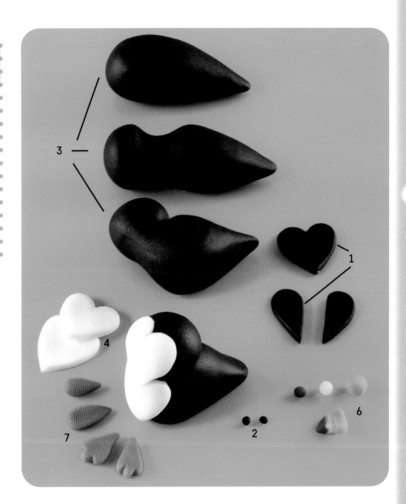

Instructions:

1 For the wings, roll out the black fondant (sugarpaste) thinly. Using the heart cutter, cut out the heart shape and then cut it in half to make two wings.

2 For the eyes, roll some black fondant (sugarpaste) into two tiny balls.

3 Form the black fondant (sugarpaste) into a 6cm (2½in) pointed cone for the body. Roll gently between your two fingers at the rounded end to make the neck and bend to stand the body up.

4 Roll out some white fondant (sugarpaste) thinly. Using the heart cutter again, cut out two hearts and stick on one for the tummy, and one above it, slightly overlapping for the face.

5 Stick the two tiny black fondant (sugarpaste) eyes and the wings in place.

6 Make a small pea-sized ball of blue fondant (sugarpaste), a smaller ball of yellow and an even smaller ball of red fondant (sugarpaste). Press them together to form the beak shape and stick the beak on to the head.

7 Roll two small pea-sized pieces of orange fondant (sugarpaste) into cone shapes, and flatten slightly. Mark on three toes with the Dresden tool or a cocktail stick and attach them under the body.

DRACULA

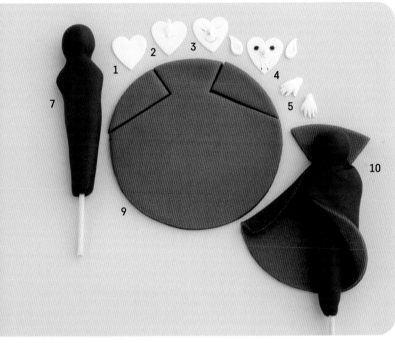

Materials:

Small amount of white
modelling paste

Red food-colouring pen

50g (1¾oz) black
modelling paste

25g (1oz) red modelling paste

Tools:

Rolling pin

2cm (¾in) heart cutter

Dresden tool

Small, fine palette knife

Smile tool (petal-veining tool or
drinking straw)

Multi-mould for small hands
and pointed ears

Food-grade kebab stick,
barbecue stick or
cake-pop stick

10cm (4in) circle cutter
or template

Ruler

43

Instructions:

1 Make the white pieces first. Roll out white modelling paste thinly. Cut out one 2cm (¾in) heart and two tiny pointed teeth. Add red food colouring to the points of the teeth.

2 Make a tiny white carrot for the nose. Stick it on to the face pointing upwards. Press the Dresden tool in to make nostrils. Curve the nose downwards.

3 Mark the eyes and eyebrows with the end of the small, fine palette knife. Make two tiny black eyes and stick them in place.

4 Mark the mouth with the smile tool. Attach the teeth by pressing them on to the dampened mouth.

5 Make two small, white hands and two white ears using the multi-mould.

6 Keep the white items covered or in a plastic bag to keep them soft until you are ready to stick them on.

7 For the body, use 25g (1oz) of black modelling paste to make a 10cm (4in) long carrot shape.
Push the stick in through the pointed end. Push it up as far as it will go without coming out. Reshape if necessary.

8 Roll between your fingers a short way down from the rounded end to make the neck and shoulders. Pinch the shoulders outwards slightly and flatten the chest.

9 For the cape, roll out the black and red modelling paste thinly. Cut out a red 10cm (4in) circle and place it on top of the black paste. Roll again

to join the layers. Cut again with the 10cm (4in) circle cutter. Cut right-angles out as shown (use a large, square cutter or a knife and ruler).

10 Dampen the back of the neck and body. Lay it on the red side of the cape. Make sure that it sticks to the neck and shoulders. Dampen the edges of the cape to form sleeves. Bring one over the front of the body to the shoulder. Insert a hand under the edge of the cape.

11 Fold over the other edge of the cape and insert the other hand.

12 Flick the front edge of the cape back to reveal the red lining.

13 Stick on the face and ears.

14 Leave to dry until the cape holds its shape.

KITTEN SLIPPER

Materials:

Mexican (flower/gum) paste
  in pink

Pink fondant (sugarpaste) for
  the fluff

Tools:

Small non-stick rolling pin

1cm (⅜in) and 2.5cm (1in)
  circle cutters

4cm (1½in) shoe sole cutter

Dowel

Tea strainer/sieve

Small fine palette knife

Dresden tool

Waterbrush/small paintbrush and water

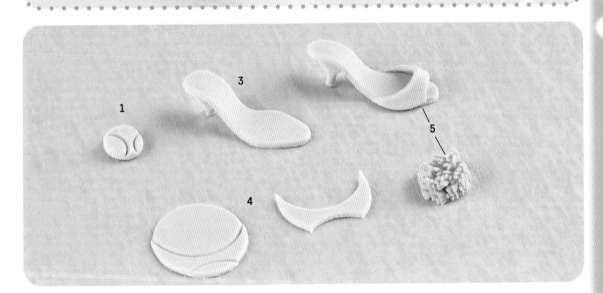

Instructions:

1 For the heel, roll out the paste to a thickness of 2mm (¹⁄₁₀in). Cut out a 1cm (⅜in) circle. Use the same circle cutter to cut across the middle to form the back curve of the heel. Cut again to form the front curve. Allow the heel to dry for a few minutes, turning it over occasionally.

2 To make the sole, roll the Mexican paste to a thickness of 1mm (¹⁄₂₀in). Cut out the 4cm (1½in) sole. Rest the heel end of the sole over a dowel for a few minutes to create the high-heeled shape, until the sole feels leathery.

3 Dampen the top curve of the heel and attach under the sole. Lay the slipper on its side and cut a tiny piece off the point of the heel to enable it to stand straight. Stand the shoe up and allow to dry for at least 30 minutes.

4 Roll out the Mexican paste thinly. Allow to dry slightly on each side until the paste feels leathery. Cut out a 2.5cm (1in) circle. Use the same cutter to cut a tiny curve off for the toe end, and a larger piece off the other side of the circle. Dampen the underside edges of the shape, stick to the sides of the sole and allow to dry for 30 minutes.

5 To make the fluff, press small pea-sized pieces of pink fondant (sugarpaste) through a tea strainer or sieve with your thumb or finger. Use the palette knife to remove the fluff. Dampen the surface of the toe piece. Use the Dresden tool or cocktail stick to attach the fluff without flattening it.

6 Stand the slipper up and allow it to dry.

FOOTBALL

Materials:

- Modelling paste in flesh, white, red, brown and black
- Chocolate football or football cake decoration
- Sugar glue
- Edible ink pen in black or brown

Tools:

- Marzipan/plastic spacers, 1.3cm (½in) depth
- Non-stick rolling pin
- Circle cutter, 2.5cm (1in)
- Square cutter, 4cm (1½in)
- Smoother

- Bulbous cone tool
- Cutting wheel
- Mini scallop tool
- Ball tool/mini ball tool
- Piping tube no. 3
- Blossom plunger, 1cm (⅜in)
- Food bag
- Craft knife
- Scriber
- Leaf veining tool
- Small paintbrush

Back of the Net

Make your footballer a member of the team you support by changing the colour of his or her shirt. Bend the limbs in different positions to put your player in some dynamic, goal-scoring poses and recreate a scene on your cake. Here I have used drinking straws for the goal posts and coconut dyed green with food colouring for the grass.

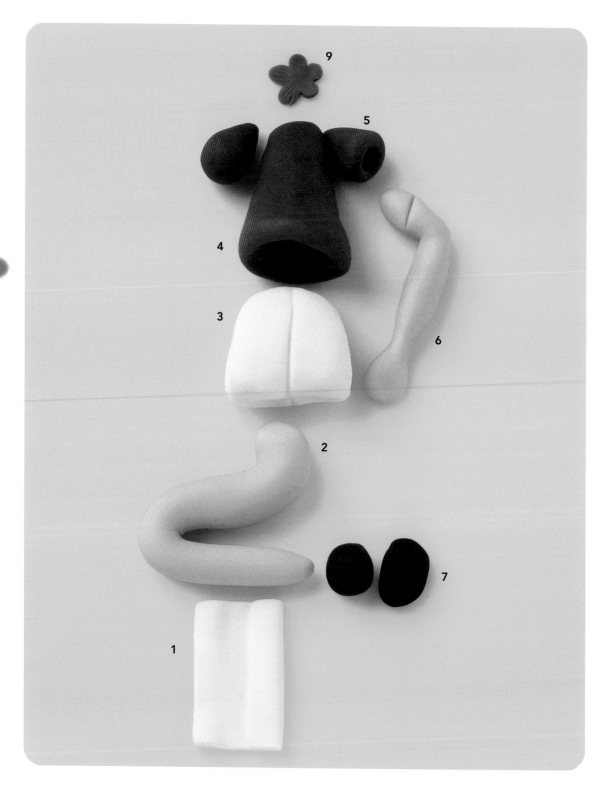

Instructions:

1 To make the socks, roll out some white modelling paste and cut out two squares with the 4cm (1½in) cutter. Fold over one edge on each to make a turnover. Place both in a food bag.

2 For the legs, cut out two circles of the flesh-coloured paste. Roll each into a long sausage shape about 10cm (4in) long, one for each leg. Secure a sock to the end of each leg and bend into a kneeling position, moulding the top for a waist.

3 For the shorts, roll two circles of white paste into an oval shape, flatten slightly with the smoother and shape to a rectangle with rounded edges. Hollow out the bottom end of the shorts slightly with the bulbous cone tool, run a cutting wheel down the middle of the shorts for a seam and secure to the tops of the legs (waist end) with sugar glue.

4 To make the football shirt, roll two circles of red paste into a pear shape. Push your thumb into the wide end to make a hollow and secure to the shorts.

5 For each shirt sleeve, roll a quarter of a circle into a cone shape. Indent the wide end with the ball tool (so that it will be easier to attach to the arm) and secure to each side of the top of the shirt (pointed end at the top).

6 Use half a circle of flesh-coloured modelling paste per arm, rolled into an oval. Use your fingers to lengthen the oval; place it on your work surface and roll it back and forth into a sausage shape. Place your little finger on the areas where the elbows will be and and roll back and forth on the work surface. This will thin the paste to define these areas. Pinch to create bends. Use a smoother to remove any finger marks, but do not squash. Attach to the sleeves with sugar glue.

7 Use an eighth of a circle of black paste per shoe and roll into an oval shape. Mark with the cutting wheel to define the heel and sole. Position them at the base of each leg.

8 For the head, cut out a half circle of flesh-coloured paste and roll into a ball. Using a mini ball tool, approximately in the centre of the ball, make a recess for the nose. Push the tool lightly into the paste ball. To add colour to the cheeks, apply edible dust sparingly with a very small soft paintbrush; remove the excess on a piece of kitchen paper first. Attach to the top of the shirt with sugar glue.

9 For the mouth, Push a mini scallop tool into the paste to make a smile or frown and use a craft knife to add the corners of the mouth.

10 For the ears, roll out some paste thinly and use no. 3 or 4 piping tubes to cut out a circle. Roll it into a ball and cut it in half to make two ears. Attach one at each side of the head, using sugar glue.

11 For the nose roll out some paste thinly and use no. 3 or 4 piping tubes to cut out a circle. Roll into a ball and secure into the recess in the centre of the head, using sugar glue.

12 Draw on the eyes and eyebrows with the edible ink pen. Alternatively, for the eyes, roll out some white paste thinly, and using a no. 3 piping tube cut out two very small circles and sugar glue them on to the head. Leave to dry before marking on the pupils with an edible ink pen.

13 For the hair, roll out a small amount of brown paste and cut out a flower shape with the 1cm (⅜in) blossom plunger. Add texture using the leaf veining tool and secure it to the top of the head with sugar glue.

DACHSHUND

Instructions:

1 Shape 10g (⅓oz) of paste to a 6cm (2⅜in) sausage for the body. Push a short candy stick vertically through the sausage at the neck end. Make a tiny short pointed cone for the tail and stick it on.

2 Cut 2g (1/12oz) of paste into four equal pieces for the legs. Roll each to form a 2cm (¾in) sausage. Curve each leg and mark toes with a knife.

3 Attach the legs to the sides of the body with all the toe ends pointing forwards.

4 Shape 2.5g (1/10oz) paste to a long pear shape. Shape the fat end of the head to form a high forehead. Mark the eyes and nose with a Dresden tool. Insert edible black sugar pearls for the eyes and nose. Mark the mouth using a knife.

5 Make two very tiny sausages of paste and attach over the eyes.

6 Roll out the paste thinly and cut out two small oval shapes for ears. Attach them to the top of the head facing backwards, and then fold them over to look floppy, as shown opposite.

Ben
This lovely scarf and hat will keep Ben warm. You might try a different textured rolling pin or colour for the scarf.

PENGUIN

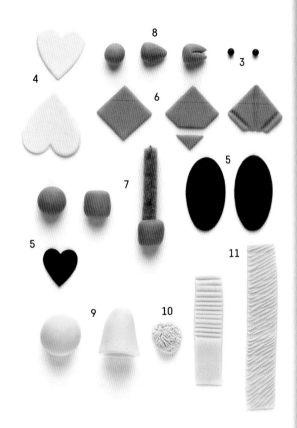

Materials:

75g (2½oz) black modelling paste

12g (½oz) orange modelling paste

30g (1oz) pale blue modelling paste

Small amount of white modelling paste

Two small black sugar balls

One orange chenille stick

Cocktail stick

Tools:

Cutters: small and medium hearts, small 1.5cm (⅝in) square, medium 4.5cm (1¾in) oval

Sugar glue

Sieve

Textured rolling pin (diagonal stripes)

Instructions:

1 Make a basic body in black as shown on page 20, and insert an 8cm (3¼in) cocktail stick. Make two holes at the front for the legs with the pointed tool.

2 Roll 20g (⅔oz) of black paste into a ball for the head. Using a little sugar glue, attach it to the body.

3 Cut out one small and one medium heart shape from the white paste, and glue the small heart on to the front of the face. Use the pointed tool to make one hole for the beak and two holes for the eyes. Insert the black sugar balls into the eyeholes.

4 Glue the medium white heart on to the body as shown in the photograph opposite.

5 Using the black paste, cut out two medium ovals and one small heart. Attach the oval arms at the back of the body with a little sugar glue before bringing them forward as shown, supporting them with foam if necessary. Attach the small heart at the back of the body with a little glue and point it upwards for the tail.

6 Use the small square cutter to cut out two squares from the orange paste for the feet. Cut off one small corner from each. Mark each foot with a cocktail stick as shown.

Roll 5g (⅛oz) of orange paste into a ball, then cut it in two. Roll each half into a ball and place one on top of each foot using a little sugar glue.

7 Cut a 7.5cm (3in) length of chenille stick and add sugar glue to each end. Attach a foot to one end and insert the other end into the body. Repeat for the other leg and foot.

8 For the beak, roll 1.5g (¹⁄₁₆oz) of orange paste into a ball and shape as shown. Cut halfway down the paste, then attach to the front of the face with a little glue.

9 For the bobble hat, roll 10g (⅓oz) of pale blue paste into a ball, then into a small cone shape. Using sugar glue, attach it to the top of the head. Roll out a thin strip of paste to go around the hat, and mark it with a cocktail stick. Attach the strip to the hat with sugar glue.

10 For the bobble, push a little paste through a sieve to make a ball, and attach it to the hat with sugar glue.

11 For the scarf, roll out a long strip of pale blue paste, not too thinly, then roll over it with the textured rolling pin. Cut the piece to size, wrap it around the penguin, then secure it in place with sugar glue. Snip the ends with scissors to make the tassels, and leave it to dry.

Make a baby hippopotamus by reducing all the sizes and using pink fondant (sugarpaste).

HIPPOPOTAMUS

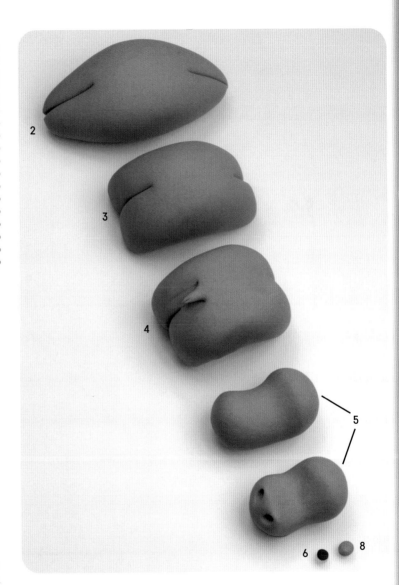

Materials:

50g (1¾oz) purple
    fondant (sugarpaste)

Tiny pieces of white and black
    fondant (sugarpaste)

Candy stick

Tools:

Thin palette knife

Sharp pointed scissors

Cocktail stick

Instructions:

1 Divide the paste; about 15g (½oz) for the head and ears, and 35g (1¼oz) for the body. To make the body, shape a ball of purple paste in the palm of your hand to form a long oval.

2 Cut into the narrow ends to make the legs.

3 Bend the whole body to form a curve, and to stand upright on the legs. Push a candy stick in at the top of the front legs to support the head (not shown).

4 Snip a small tail with scissors.

5 For the head, break off a tiny piece of paste and save it to make the ears. Make a fat pear shape for the head. Mark two nostrils, and mark the mouth using a knife.

6 For the eyes, make two tiny, flattened balls of white (not shown), and press on two smaller balls of black. Stick on to the face.

7 Attach the head on to the body.

8 Make two tiny balls for the ears from the remaining purple fondant (sugarpaste). Shape the indents and attach the ears to the head.

HANDSOME GROOM

Materials:

- Modelling paste: flesh-coloured: 13g (½oz); black: 63g (2¹⁄₁₀oz); white: pea-sized ball; red: pea-sized ball
- Sugar/spaghetti sticks
- Edible glue/pasteurised egg white
- White and black gel food colouring

Tools:

Cutting mat

Non-stick rolling pin

Scalpel/craft knife

Small paintbrush

Piping nozzle (tube)

Toothpick

Dresden tool/skewer

Instructions:

1 Make a head and face, using black paste for the eyes, as described in steps 1–5, page 31.

2 Make trousers from 20g (⅔oz) of black paste rolled into a sausage 14cm(5⅔in) long, rolling the middle of the sausage slightly narrower than the ends. Fold the sausage in half to form trouser legs and cut the rounded top of the trousers level with a scalpel, craft knife or blade, keeping the top of the legs intact. The trousers should be 6cm (2⅓in) long.

3 Roll 3g (¹⁄₁₀oz) of black paste into two ovals and attach them to the bottom of the trouser legs to make shoes. Stick two sugar sticks/uncooked spaghetti through the legs into the feet, protruding 1.5cm (⅗in) above the trousers.

4 To make the jacket roll 20g (⅔oz) of paste into a large, thick cone. Flatten the cone on your workbench and cut it off at the widest end. It should be 3.5cm (1½in) long. Indent the top of the cone with a Dresden tool/skewer where the neck and shirt will be attached. Mark a vertical line down the centre of the jacket and press the tip of a piping nozzle into the paste next to the line to resemble buttons. Push the jacket onto the trousers and glue it with edible glue. Stick a sugar stick/spaghetti through leaving a piece 1.5cm (⅗in) long protruding above the jacket.

5 Roll a pea-sized piece of flesh-coloured paste into a thick sausage. Place the sausage onto the protruding sugar stick or spaghetti to make a neck.

6 Roll out a pea-sized piece of white paste until very thin. Cut out one long triangle to form the shirt and cut two small triangles to form the collar. Attach them to the jacket and neck with edible glue/egg white.

7 Roll out 3g (¹⁄₁₀oz) of black paste and cut out one long rectangle to fit around the neck, of 4.5cm (1¾in). Cut off the corners diagonally and attach it around the neck to form a collar. Cut two smaller narrow triangles and attach them to the front of the jacket to make lapels.

8 Roll 10g (⅓oz) of black paste into two sausages, each 4.5cm (1¾in) long to make sleeves. Make a hole in one end of each sausage by pushing a skewer into the paste where the hands will be attached. Attach the arms to the sides of the body with a drop of edible glue/egg white. Indent the sleeves here and there with a Dresden tool/skewer to make creases.

9 Make hands from a pea-sized ball of flesh-coloured paste rolled into two elongated cones. Roll the cones between your index fingers to make wrists. Flatten the wider end of each cone and push the narrow end into the sleeves, attaching it with a drop of edible glue/egg white.

10 Attach the dried head to the neck and leave to dry for a few hours or overnight before attaching the hair.

11 Roll small tapered sausages from 5g (¹⁄₆oz) of black paste. Starting at the nape of the neck, glue overlapping random sausages all the way over the head to the forehead. Place a few hair strands in front of the ears. Place one tapered sausage in front of each ear, towards the jaw line, to make sideburns; mark with a knife.

12 For the tie, roll out the red paste and cut it into a thin rectangular strip to form a tie. Fold back two corners of the strip to form a triangle at the top of the tie and cut off the opposite two corners to form the bottom of the tie. Attach the tie to the groom's shirt with a drop of edible glue/egg white. For the buttonhole, roll out a tiny amount of red paste until almost paper thin. Cut a thin strip and roll it up to form a tiny rose. Attach it to the groom's jacket.

Glamour Girl
Make an alternative bag in pure white with white sparkles. These bags would look perfect on a cake for someone with an eye for glamorous accessories.

RED GLITTER BAG

Materials:

Mexican (flower/gum) paste in red

Edible red glitter

Piping gel

Tools:

Small, non-stick rolling pin

4cm (1½in) square cutter

0.5cm (¼in) oval cutter

Music stave cutter

Fine stitching wheel

Fine paintbrush

Instructions:

1 Roll the paste 3mm (⅛in) thick. Cut out two 5mm (¼in) ovals. Leave to dry.

2 Roll the paste thinly. Cut one 4cm (1½in) square and one strip using the music stave cutter.

3 Dampen along two sides of the square. Stand the ovals up on their ends about halfway down the sides of the square. Bring the bottom flap up over the edges of the ovals and then bring the top flap over to overlap the bottom flap.

4 Mark along the strip with the fine stitching wheel. Attach the ends to the sides of the bag.

5 For best results, allow the surface of the bag to dry before sticking the glitter on. Lay the bag on a piece of paper or plastic, so that the excess glitter can be poured back into the jar. Spread a thin layer of piping gel on the top flap of the bag. Sprinkle the edible glitter on to it. Use a dry paintbrush to brush away the excess glitter.

Beryl
A purple bow makes a great alternative.

SHEEP

Materials:

- 100g (3½oz) white modelling paste
- 60g (2⅛oz) black modelling paste
- Small amount of pink Mexican (flower/gum) paste
- Two white stamens
- One black chenille stick
- Cocktail sticks
- White wool

Tools:

- Pointed tool
- Smiley tool/drinking straw
- Paintbrushes
- Texture frilling tool
- Ball tool
- Small, non-stick rolling pin)
- Thin palette knife
- Cutters: small oval, small circle
- Small pair of scissors
- Fine black fibre-tip pen
- Sugar glue
- Rolling pin

2 & 11

3

10

5

11

7

6

8

12

Instructions:

1 Make a basic body in white as shown on page 20, insert a cocktail stick and make two holes in the front for the legs using the pointed tool.

2 For the fur, roll out the remaining 45g (1½oz) of white paste, not too thinly. Cut out small circles and roll each one into a ball, making them the same size. Starting at the base of the body glue them on individually in rows; continue going up the body until you reach the top. Try not to leave any gaps between the balls.

3 Create the head by rolling 20g (⅔oz) of black fondant (sugarpaste) into a ball and then into an oval. Make two holes for the nose.

4 Mark the mouth with the small circle cutter and use a pointed tool to make a small hole at each end.

5 For the eyes, roll 3g (⅛oz) of black paste into two balls. Using the pointed tool, make a hole in the middle, push in a stamen and mark it with a black pen. Attach the eyes to the top of the head with a little glue.

6 Cut a chenille stick in half and one piece in half again, making two 7.5cm (3in) legs and one 15cm (6in) arm length.

7 Make the hooves by rolling 16g (½oz) of black paste into a ball. Cut it in half and make two cones, then use a palette knife to mark a line down the front of each one. Add a little sugar glue to the ends of each 7.5cm (3in) chenille stick, attach one hoof to one end and insert the other end into the body at the front. Repeat for the other leg. Bend into shape when dry.

8 For the arms and hands, roll 5g (⅙oz) of black paste into a ball then cut it in half with scissors. Roll each half into a pear shape. Add sugar glue to each end of the 15cm (6in) chenille stick and attach the hands. Bend the chenille stick round the back of the cocktail stick and glue it in place, bringing the arms and hands in front.

9 Push the head on to the cocktail stick using a little sugar glue.

10 Use the small oval cutter to cut out two ears from black paste. Attach them to the top of the head with a little glue, supporting them with foam if necessary.

11 Following the instructions for step 2, make several small white balls and glue them on the top of the ears until the top of the head is covered. When dry, roll out some pink Mexican paste and make a bow out of it. Secure this on top of the balls.

12 Roll a small piece of black paste into a cone, and glue it into place as a tail.

13 Make the knitting on cocktail sticks, using white wool, then attach it to the hands while the paste is still soft.

VIOLA

Materials:

Mexican (flower/gum) paste
  in white

Paste food colour: black

White alcohol

Powdered food colour: yellow,
  purple, orange

Royal icing: gooseberry green

Tools:

Small five-petal blossom cutter:
  30mm (1¼in)

Large oval plaque cutter:
  70mm (2¾in)

Ball tool

Paintbrushes: size 2/0 round,
  12mm (½in) flat

Piping bag and leaf tube: ST52

Mini modelling tool

Mexican foam balling pad

Pearl lustre spray with spray
  gun attachment

Instructions:

1 On a non-stick surface, roll out some white Mexican paste quite thinly. Cut one five-petal blossom shape using the five-petal blossom cutter (A).

2 Lay a mini modelling tool horizontally across the base of one of the top petals and roll across the surface towards the top of the petal to elongate. Now place the same tool vertically down the centre of the petal with the tip of the tool at the centre of the flower and roll from side to side to widen the petal (B). Repeat for the second top petal.

3 Repeat the process at step 2 for the bottom petal (the one directly opposite the top two petals), but this time lengthen a little and widen a lot more (C).

4 The two side petals are just widened, not lengthened, as described above in step 2. Place the flower on to a Mexican foam balling pad and rub around the outside edge of each petal with a ball tool to soften. Push the ball tool into the centre of each petal to cup (D).

5 Pull the petals into shape with your fingers, overlap the top two petals slightly, pull the side petals forward and the bottom petal forward, pinching it to a soft point at the base. Leave on scrunched-up kitchen paper to dry. To colour, use the flat brush with some yellow powdered food colour. Pull the colour over the outer edge of the petal in towards the centre, continuing over the bottom petal and across the bottom half of the two side petals (E).

6 Brush some purple powdered food colour over the top two petals and blend across the top half of the side petals (F). Mix some black paste food colour with a little white alcohol and use the size 2/0 paintbrush to paint some lines on to the bottom and side petals.

7 With royal icing, arrange on an oval plaque, sprayed with pearl lustre spray. Pipe leaves with green royal icing and the leaf tube, ensuring the deep 'V' of the piping tube faces the sides (G).

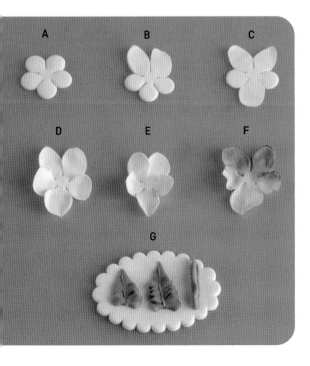

BLOSSOM FAIRY

Materials:

10g (⅓oz) flesh-coloured fondant (sugarpaste) for the head

White fondant (sugarpaste); 10g (⅓oz) for the body, 10g (⅓oz) for the hands and feet

10g (⅓oz) white modelling paste for the wings and blossoms

Five candy sticks

Tiny amount of black fondant (sugarpaste) for the eyes

Tools:

Non-stick rolling pin

Small butterfly cutter

Large and tiny blossom cutters

Small drinking straw

Thin palette knife

Plastic sandwich bag

Water brush

Dresden tool or cocktail stick

Tissue paper

Instructions:

1 Cut out the wings using white modelling paste with a small butterfly cutter. Leave to dry overnight.

2 Use two candy sticks for the legs. For the shoes, make two pea-sized pieces of white fondant (sugarpaste) and shape each to a point. Dampen the ends of the legs and attach the shoes.

3 For the arms, cut two candy sticks to make them slightly shorter than the legs. For the hands, make two pea-sized pieces of white fondant (sugarpaste) to form simple hand shapes and cut out a tiny triangle from each to form thumbs. Dampen the ends of the arms and attach the hands.

4 Make an egg shape from white fondant (sugarpaste) for the body, with a candy stick for support, slightly sticking out. Dampen the top ends of the legs and arms and push them into the body.

5 For the head, take the flesh-coloured fondant (sugarpaste) and pinch off a piece. Use this to make two tiny teardrop shapes for the ears and a tiny pinhead piece for the nose. Form the rest into a ball and use a finger to roll a slight indentation across the middle. Make a hole in the neck end using a dry candy stick. Attach the nose in the centre of the face, and press a mouth shape with the cut drinking straw under the nose. Dampen the sides of the head in line with the nose. Stick the ears on and press in place using a Dresden tool or cocktail stick, forming the ear shape. Make two tiny pinhead size pieces of black fondant (sugarpaste) for the eyes. Dampen the face to stick them on, slightly above the nose. Dampen the end of the candy stick neck, and attach the head.

6 Roll out white modelling paste thinly. Dampen around the bottom of the body and the top of the arms, cut out large blossoms and stick them in place. Dampen the fairy's head and attach tiny blossoms to it. Stick a blossom on each foot.

7 Attach the wings with thick edible glue (gunge). Prop them up with scrunched-up tissue paper until the glue is dry.

OWL

Materials:
- 25g (just under 1oz) brown or chocolate fondant (sugarpaste)
- Small amounts of white, pale brown and black fondant (sugarpaste)

Tools:
- Small sharp-pointed scissors
- Small sieve/sugarcraft gun
- Heart cutter: 2.5cm (1in)
- Circle cutters: 2cm (¾in) and 1cm (⅜in)
- Small rolling pin

Instructions:

1 To make the beak, form a tiny cone from brown fondant (sugarpaste).

2 For the two wings, model each from a large pea-sized piece of brown paste and make into a fat carrot shape. Flatten slightly and mark on the feathers using the Dresden tool.

3 To make the body, roll the main piece of brown fondant (sugarpaste) into an oval shape, then roll it between your two fingers to form the neck and the head. Gently pinch and stroke the other end to form a short tail.

4 Cut out a heart from some thinly rolled-out white fondant (sugarpaste) and stick on the body for a tummy. Use fine sharp-pointed scissors (with points towards the feet of the owl) to snip through the surface of the paste on the tummy to form lots of little spikes. Stroke the spikes downwards to look like feathers. When snipping with the scissors the underneath colour will then show.

5 Attach the wings to the sides of the body.

6 To make the face, roll out white paste thinly. Cut out a 2cm (¾in) and a 1cm (⅜in) circle. Cut each circle into quarters, attach one of the larger quarters for the chin and mark with the Dresden tool to suggest feathers. For the eye area, roll out some pale brown paste. Cut out a 2cm (¾in) circle and cut it into quarters. Stick two of the small white quarters to the pale brown ones. Stick on two small eyes made from two balls of black fondant (sugarpaste). Attach these two quarters and a plain quarter for the forehead, to the face. Mark the forehead with lines radiating outwards using the Dresden tool.

7 Attach the tiny brown beak.

8 Make two small pieces of white fluff by pressing some fondant (sugarpaste) through a sieve, sugarcraft gun, or garlic press. Stick it on to the head to look like the owl's ears.

As Wise as an Owl
Try using white fondant (sugarpaste) instead of chocolate brown. When rolling out the paste for the tummy feathers, roll out white and pale brown, press together and roll again. Cut out the heart shape and stick to the tummy with the pale brown stuck to the body. When snipping with the scissors, the colour will then show.

GRUESOME GARGOYLE

Materials:

50g (1¾oz) stone-coloured
    modelling paste

Dark brown edible food
    colour powder

Tools:

Multi-mould for bird wings

Small, fine-pointed scissors

No. 16 (4mm) piping tube

Cocktail stick

Dresden tool

Dusting brush

Small, fine palette knife

Cutting wheel

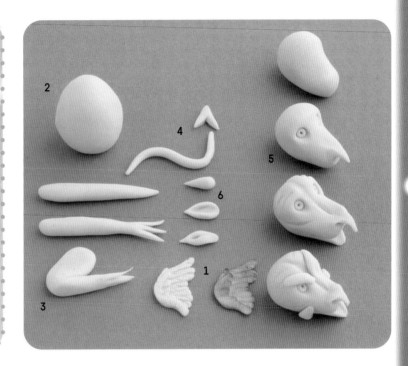

Instructions:

1 Make one pair of wings from modelling paste and leave to dry.

2 Make the body by shaping 20g (¾oz) of modelling paste into an egg shape. Stand it upright.

3 For the legs, make four 5cm (2in) long carrots using 2g (¹⁄₁₆oz) for each leg. Use the cutting wheel to cut three claws into the pointed end of each leg. Use the fine palette knife to release the legs from the work surface as the pointed toes will be delicate. Roll up two of the legs from the fatter end and flatten them slightly. Stick these to the base of the body for the back legs, toes facing forwards. Stick the remaining two legs to the front of the body with the toes bent forwards.

4 Roll a small pea-sized piece of modelling paste out to a thin 6cm (2¼in) sausage for the tail. Shape a tiny piece of paste into a triangle and cut a 'v' into it. Attach the triangle to the end of the tail. Attach the tail to the body.

5 Make a 10g (⅜oz) pear shape for the head. Pinch to make a very pointed nose. Cut the mouth with scissors. Mark the eyes using the piping tube and make a cocktail-stick hole in the middle. Mark the nostrils, wrinkles and mouth with the Dresden tool. Add tiny, thin sausages of paste for the eyebrows and cheeks and stick them in position.

6 Make two ears using two tiny carrot shapes. Flatten them in the middle with the Dresden tool. Pinch the base of each together and stick them on the back of the head.

7 Brush gently with dark brown edible food colour powder all over the body and wings to give the appearance of weathered stone.

8 Attach the wings. Mix a tiny pea-sized piece of modelling paste with a couple of drops of water to make a thick glue. Put a little on each wing and stick them to the back of the body. Prop up the wings if necessary while drying.

STRAPPY SANDAL

Materials:

Mexican (flower/gum) paste in
    white and bright pink
Edible glitter
Tiny silver balls
Piping gel/edible glue

Tools:

Small non-stick rolling pin
4cm (1½in) shoe sole cutter
1.5cm (⅝in) and 2.5cm (1in)
    circle cutters
Dowel
Music stave cutter
Dresden tool
Small fine palette knife
Small sharp pointed scissors
Waterbrush/small paintbrush
    and water

Instructions:

1 For the heel, roll out the pink paste to a thickness of 2mm (1/10 in). Cut the paste using the 1.5cm (⅝in) circle cutter. Use the 2.5cm (1in) circle cutter to cut across the middle to form the back curve of the heel. Cut again using the 1.5cm (⅝in) circle to form the front curve. Allow the heel to dry for a few minutes, turning it over occasionally.

2 Roll the pink paste to a thickness of 1mm (½0in). Cut out the 4cm (1½in) sole. Rest the heel end of the sole over a dowel for a few minutes to make the high-heeled shape, until the sole feels leathery.

3 Dampen the top curve of the heel and attach under the sole. Lay the shoe on its side and cut a tiny piece off the point of the heel using the palette knife to enable it to stand straight. Stand the shoe up and allow to dry for at least 30 minutes.

4 Roll out the white paste thinly. Allow to dry slightly on each side until the paste feels leathery. Cut the straps using the music stave cutter. Loop one strap as shown and dampen where the strap crosses to attach it to itself.

5 Dampen the side edges of the front end of the sole. Press one strap to the sides, overhanging the edges. Repeat, crossing over the top of the first strap. Lay the shoe on its side and cut off the excess strap ends with the scissors.

6 Dampen the side edges of the heel end of the sole. Take the strap from step 4. Press the ends to the sides of the sole, overlapping the edges and holding the loop forwards. Cut the excess off as in step 5.

7 Stand the shoe up and allow to dry, until dry enough to hold by the heel.

8 Brush piping gel or edible glue over the straps. Sprinkle with edible glitter. Use a small, dry paintbrush or cotton bud to remove any excess glitter.

9 Attach tiny silver balls with piping gel or edible glue.

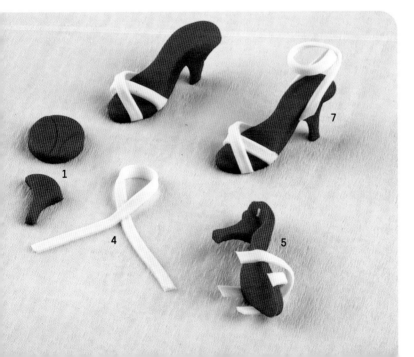

Go Girls!
Capturing the essence of sun, fun and games on the beach, these girls love to volley the day away!

BEACH VOLLEYBALL

Materials:

Modelling paste: flesh, pink, white, black, plus any three colours of your choice for the ball

Edible ink pens in black and blue

Edible red dust

Popsicle (lollipop) sticks

Sugar glue

Tools:

Marzipan/plastic spacers, 1.3cm (½in) depth

Non-stick rolling pin

Craft knife

Circle cutter, 2.5cm (1in)

Ball tool and mini ball tool

Mini scallop tool

Smoother

Piping tube no. 3

Small paintbrush

Kitchen paper

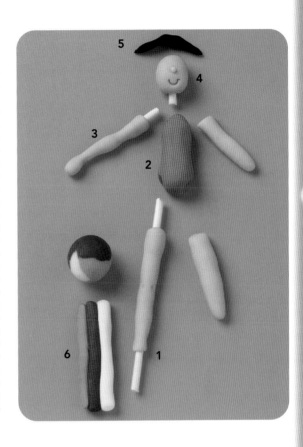

Instructions:

1 For the legs, take one flesh-coloured circle of paste, cut it in half and roll each half into a sausage shape 6.5cm (2½in) long. Insert a popsicle stick into the top and the bottom of each leg. Using the mini ball tool, mark two indentations on to the knee cap. There are no feet to model for this project.

2 For the body, use one circle of pink paste and roll it into an oval shape. Indent the leg and arm sockets with the ball tool.

3 For the arms, cut one circle of flesh-coloured paste in half and follow the instructions in step 6, page

49. Insert a popsicle stick through the length of each arm.

4 To make the head, take a circle of flesh-coloured paste and follow the instructions in step 8, page 49. For the nose and mouth follow steps 9 and 11 on page 49 and either draw on the eyes with the black edible ink pen, or roll out some white paste, and using a no. 3 piping tube, cut out two small circles and sugar glue them to the head. Draw on pupils with an edible ink pen.

5 To make the hair, take a small amount of black paste and model into teardrop shapes. Stick these

randomly on the head with sugar glue, with some sticking up at various angles for movement. Leave the model to dry flat at least overnight.

6 To make the volleyball, take three different colours of leftover paste, roll them to size between the spacers and cut out one circle of each colour. Roll each circle into a sausage shape and roll them altogether into a ball. Leave to dry overnight. Your volleyball players will stand up if you insert the popsicle sticks into a cake. Decorate the cake with brown sugar to give the impression of a sandy beach.

SCHNAUZER

Materials:

- 30g (1oz) green modelling paste
- Edible sugar candy sticks painted grey with black food colour
- 15g (½oz) grey modelling paste
- Small amount of pale grey fondant (sugarpaste) for fluff
- Edible black sugar pearls
- Clear piping gel (optional)

Tools:

- Small petal cutter
- Dresden tool
- Water brush
- Thin palette knife
- Tea strainer/small sieve

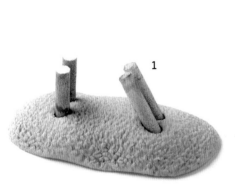

Instructions:

1 Shape the green paste to a 6cm (2⅜in) oval for the base and texture the surface to look like grass using the Dresden tool. Push in two 3cm (1¼in) candy sticks at an angle as shown, then two vertically, with 3cm (1¼in) between the front and back pairs to allow space for the body to stick on. Trim the tops of the vertical legs to be level with the top of the back legs.

2 Shape 10g (⅓oz) of grey paste to a 3cm (1¼in) cone for the body. Pinch and shape a small vertical tail at the narrow end. Push in an edible candy stick vertically for the neck. Dampen the tops of the legs and push the

body into place, head end above the vertical legs.

3 Shape 2.5g (¹⁄₁₀oz) of grey paste to a long pear shape. Turn up the narrow end slightly for the nose. Pinch and shape the sides of the muzzle to make them hang down more. Shape the fat end of the head gently to form a higher forehead. Mark the eyes and nose with a Dresden tool and insert edible black sugar pearls. Dampen the top of the neck and press the head into place.

4 Roll out the paste thinly and cut out two small petal shapes for the ears. Attach them to the back of the head

with the points upwards, and then fold them over and form them to look angled, as shown.

5 Dampen the areas at the base of the legs, cheeks, and eyebrows where the fluff will go. Push the grey fondant (sugarpaste) through a tea stainer/small sieve to make fluff. When it is the length you want, cut it off with a knife and attach it to the dampened areas on the dog. Press into place with the Dresden tool as using your fingers would flatten the fluff. If you have trouble getting it to stay on, use clear piping gel as a glue instead of dampening with water.

Harry

Harry wants it to snow so he can go skiing. The crystal effect of the white glitter has many uses.

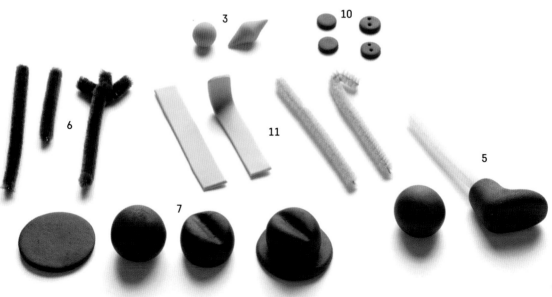

3

10

6

11

5

7

SNOWMAN

Materials:

- 65g (2¼oz) white modelling paste
- 35g (1¼oz) black modelling paste
- Small amounts of orange, blue, and grey modelling paste
- White glitter
- Two small black sugar balls
- One brown, grey and white chenille stick

Tools:

- Cutters: small and medium circle
- Sugar glue

Instructions:

1 Make a white body by rolling 45g (1½oz) of modelling paste into a ball. Shape the paste into a cone 6.5cm (2½in) tall and insert an 8cm (3¼in) cocktail stick. Make two holes for the legs. Leave to dry.

2 For the head, roll 20g (⅔oz) of white paste into a ball, then make a hole in the middle of the face for the nose and two small holes for the eyes. Insert two black sugar balls. Attach the head to the body using a little sugar glue.

3 For the nose, roll a small piece of orange paste into a ball, then make a point at each end. Insert one end into the head with a little sugar glue. Leave to dry.

4 Lightly cover the head and the body with glue. Sprinkle all over with white glitter and shake off the excess. Dust the glitter carefully from the eyes and nose, then leave to dry.

5 Cut two 7.5cm (3in) lengths of white chenille stick for the legs, then roll 20g (⅔oz) of black paste into a ball. Cut the ball in half and roll each part into a sausage shape, before turning up one end of each to make the boots, as shown. Lightly glue both ends of the chenille stick, then insert one end into the boot and the other end into the body. Repeat for the other leg.

6 For the arms, cut two 7.5cm (3in) lengths and two 2cm (¾in) lengths of brown chenille stick. Wrap and twist the smaller length around the top of the longer part as shown, then push it into the top of the body. Repeat with the other arm.

7 Cut out a 4cm (1½in) circle of black paste and roll 8g (¼oz) of black paste into a ball. Using a small amount of glue, place the ball on top of the circle of black paste. Lay the pointed tool across the top and push down. Secure the hat with a little glue on to the snowman's head.

8 Roll out a thin strip of blue paste and secure it around the hat using a little glue. Turn up the front brim to finish the hat.

9 Roll out a long strip of blue paste for the scarf and wrap it around the snowman, bringing one end to either side. Secure it in place with a little glue, then cut both ends to make tassels.

10 Cut out three small black circles for the buttons, attach with a little sugar glue, and mark each centre with a pointed tool as shown.

11 Roll 1.5cm x 8cm (⅝in x 3¼in) rectangles of grey paste to make the skis. Using a little glue, attach them to the bottom of the boots as shown, then slightly turn the tops over. For the ski poles, cut two 5cm (2in) lengths of grey chenille stick, turn over the tops and hook one on to each hand.

Make a baby dolphin to swim alongside its mother, using purple fondant (sugarpaste).

DOLPHIN

Materials:

15g (½oz) each of blue and pale blue fondant (sugarpaste)

Tiny piece of black fondant (sugarpaste)

Tools:

Sharp pointed scissors or thin palette knife

Cocktail stick

Instructions:

1 For the fins, shape three small pea-sized pieces of blue paste into small carrot shapes. Flatten and curve them slightly.

2 Make a smooth ball from the blue paste and one from the pale blue paste. Roll each between your hands to form pointed sausage shapes. Join them gently together by rolling.

3 Roll one end of the dolphin between your fingers to form the narrow nose. To make the tail, roll the other end of the dolphin between your fingers and flatten it slightly.

4 Cut into the centre of the flattened end about 1cm (⅜in) with the scissors or knife. Flatten and shape the points of the tail.

5 Attach one of the fins on the back and one on each side. Curve the tips towards the tail. Mark a blowhole with a cocktail stick.

6 Make the eyes from two tiny balls of black paste and attach them.

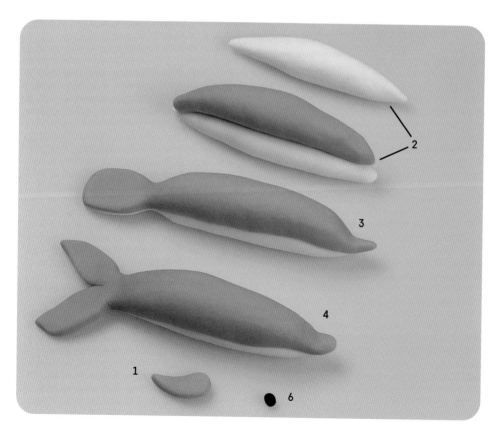

SWEET BRIDE

Materials:

Modelling paste: flesh-coloured:
   13g (½oz), blue: pinhead-sized
   piece, yellow and brown mixture:
   5g (⅙oz), light pink: 65g (2⅛oz),
   light green: 3g (¹⁄₁₀oz)

Sugar/spaghetti sticks

Edible glue/pasteurised egg white

White and brown gel food colouring

Pink dusting powder

Tools:

Cutting mat

Non-stick rolling pin

Scalpel/craft knife

Piping nozzle (tube)

Small paintbrush

Frilling tool

Toothpick

Dresden tool/skewer

Instructions:

1 Make a head as described in step 1, page 31, but roll it into a cone shape. Make the eyes from blue paste and paint the eyebrows and lashes with brown gel food colouring.

2 Make the dress from 60g (2oz) of light pink paste rolled into a cone 8.5cm (3½in) long. Make a waist by rolling the cone two-thirds of the way up between your index fingers and pulling a Dresden tool/skewer from the bottom of the dress towards the waist to make pleats. Place the cone upright and indent the top with a Dresden tool/skewer. Push a long sugar stick or a few pieces of uncooked spaghetti through the cone all the way to the bottom of the dress and protruding 1.5cm (⅔in) above the dress.

3 Make shoes from 3g (¹⁄₁₀oz) of light pink paste, rolled into two ovals and attached to the bottom of the dress with edible glue.

4 Make a neck following the instructions in step 9, page 31.

5 Form arms and hands following the instructions in step 10, page 31.

6 Roll out the leftover pink paste very thinly and cut it into strips. Roll over each strip with a frilling tool or skewer to make ruffles. Attach them to the neck and shoulders of the dress with edible glue.

7 Attach the dried head to the neck.

8 Use the yellow and brown paste mixture and make a bob hairstyle with short tapered sausages, following the instructions in step 12, page 31.

9 Make tiny roses with the light green paste, by rolling up very thin strips into rose shapes. Attach the roses to the hands of the bride with a drop of edible glue.

STARRY EVENING BAG

Materials:

Mexican (flower/gum) paste in purple and white

Tiny edible gold stars

Tiny gold-coloured sugar balls

Edible gold paint

Piping gel

Tools:

Small, non-stick rolling pin

6cm (2⅜in) circle cutter

Cutting wheel

Ruler

Tweezers

Fine paintbrush

Instructions:

1 Roll the purple paste thinly. Cut out the 6cm (2⅜in) circle. Pinch small gathers around the edge.

2 Bring all the pinched edges together and press them gently until the gathers form a 2.5cm (1in) edge. Press the edge on to the surface and use the rolling pin to flatten the gathered edge. Cut straight across with the cutting wheel. Stand the bag up.

3 Roll out the white paste thinly. Cut a strip 2.5 x 1cm (1 x ⅜in). Press a line down the centre without cutting through. Fold along the line. Dampen the straight cut edge of the purple gathered bag and stick the folded white oblong over the top.

4 Paint the folded part with edible gold paint and a fine paintbrush.

5 Attach the tiny edible stars by picking up each star with tweezers and touching the star on piping gel before placing on the surface of the bag.

6 Stick two tiny gold-coloured sugar balls to the top of the bag with a little piping gel.

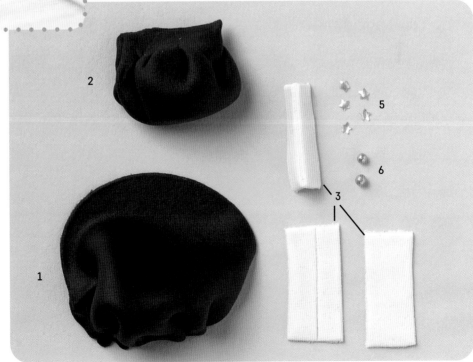

Lynne
*This chic little zebra would make
a characterful topper for any
white cake.*

ZEBRA

Materials:

80g (2⅔oz) white modelling paste

50g (1⅔oz) black modelling paste

Small amount of royal blue modelling paste

One black chenille stick

Two white stamens

Cocktail stick

Tools:

Thin palette knife

Small pair of scissors

Cutters: tiny blossom, circle

Fine black fibre-tip pen

Sugar glue

Rolling pin

Instructions:

1 Make a basic body in white as shown on page 20 and insert an 8cm (3¼in) cocktail stick. Make two holes in the front for the legs using the pointed tool.

2 Create the head by rolling 20g (⅔oz) of white paste into a ball and then into a pear shape. Make two holes for the eyes with the pointed tool. Insert stamens into the holes, then use a black pen to mark the pupils.

3 Roll out a small circle of black paste to fit over the end of the nose and use sugar glue to attach it in place as the muzzle. Make two small holes for the nostrils with the pointed tool. Mark the mouth with a circle cutter then use the pointed tool to make a hole at each end.

4 Make the hooves by rolling 25g (⅝oz) of black paste into a ball, cutting it into four and shaping each part into a cone. Use a palette knife to ark a line down the front of each one.

5 Cut a chenille stick in half and one piece in half again. You now have two 7.5cm (3in) legs and one 15cm (6in) arm length. Add sugar glue to each end of a 7.5cm (3in) length, attach a hoof to one end and insert the other end into the body at the front. Repeat for the second leg and bend each into shape when dry.

6 Add sugar glue to each end of the 15cm (6in) chenille stick and attach a hoof to each end. Bend the chenille stick round the back of the cocktail stick and glue it in place before bringing the arms and hooves to the front.

7 Push the head on to the cocktail stick, securing it with a small amount of sugar glue.

8 To make the ears, roll 2g (1⁄12oz) of white paste into a ball. Cut the ball in half, roll each piece into a ball again and push the rounded end of a pointed tool into one ball. Do not take the tool out, but glue the bottom part of the ear and place it on the top of the head firmly. Pinch the top of the paste to make a pointed ear, then remove the tool. Repeat with the other ear and leave to dry.

9 Create a mane by rolling out a strip of black paste. Snip it with scissors as shown and roll it up before lightly gluing it in place between the ears for a fluffy mane.

10 When the zebra is completely dry, mark the stripes as shown using a black pen.

11 Use the blossom cutter to make some small blue blossoms and decorate the zebra. Secure them in place with stamens.

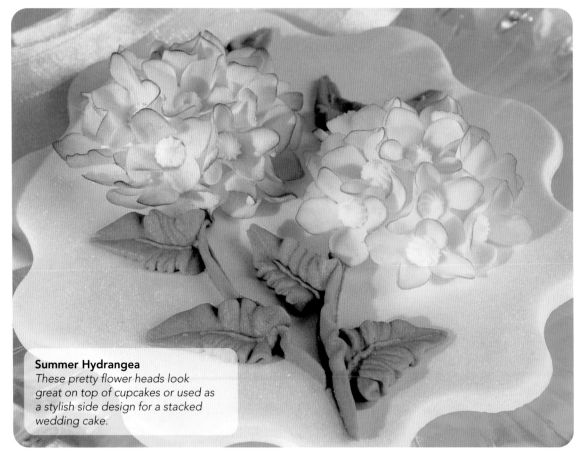

Summer Hydrangea
These pretty flower heads look great on top of cupcakes or used as a stylish side design for a stacked wedding cake.

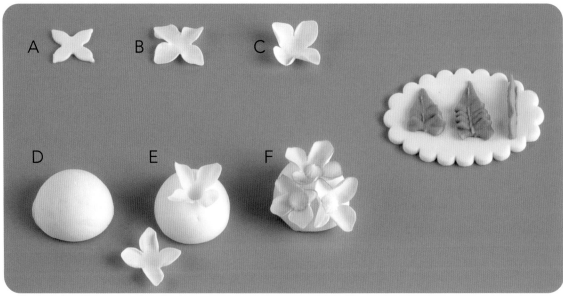

A B C

D E F

HYDRANGEA

Materials:

Mexican (flower/gum) paste
  in white

Powdered food colour: pink, blue

Royal icing: white, green

Tools:

Small daphne cutter

Round wavy-edged plaque cutter: 100mm (4in)

Half ball mould: 32mm (1¼in)

Paintbrush: 12mm (½in) flat

Piping bag, leaf tube: ST52 and rope tube: ST43

Ball tool

Pearl lustre spray with spray gun attachment

Mini modelling tool

Mexican foam balling pad

Instructions:

Flowers

1 Roll out some white Mexican paste quite thinly on a non-stick surface. Cut out a flower with a small daphne cutter (A).

2 Lay a mini modelling tool vertically down the centre of one petal, with the tip of the tool at the centre of the flower, then roll it from side to side to widen and thin the petal. Repeat for the remaining three petals (B).

3 Place the flower on to a Mexican foam modelling pad and push the ball tool into the centre of the flower to cup (C). Make several more and place inside a plastic bag to keep them soft (this will enable the flowers to fit together easily without breakage).

4 Dust the inside of the half ball mould with cornflour. Push a ball of modelling paste into the ball mould so that it fills it completely. Cut any excess paste away so that the paste is level with the edge of the mould, then remove the piece from the mould (D).

5 Use sugar glue to stick the first soft flower on to the domed centre of the half ball, pushing it into place with a ball tool (E).

6 Stick the remaining soft flowers around the half ball in the same way, and pipe a centre in each with white royal icing and the rope tube (F). Once dry, pull some blue powdered food colour softly across the edge of the petals with a flat brush to add some colour. Make a second flower in the same way, but colour this with pink rather than blue.

Leaves

7 Use royal icing to secure the flowers on a round wavy-edged plaque sprayed with pearl lustre. Pipe leaves with green royal icing and a leaf tube. Insert the tube at a 45-degree angle in between the flowers with the deep 'V' of the tube facing to the sides. Touch the surface of the plaque with the piping tube and while holding it in place gently squeeze the bag to release the icing. Whilst still squeezing, gently pull the piping bag towards you and when the leaf is large enough, stop squeezing and pull the tube quickly towards you to break the stem of icing and form the leaf tip.

8 Pipe the flower stems with green royal icing using a leaf tube. Place the tip of the tube at the base of the flowers at a 45-degree angle, with the deep 'V' of the tube facing upwards. Gently squeeze the piping bag to release the icing as you slowly pull the bag towards you. Release the squeeze on the bag and scrape the end of the tube against the surface of the plaque to finish the stem of icing.

Vibrant greens and yellows give this flower fairy a wonderfully summery feel. You could make a Michaelmas Daisy fairy with purple petals.

DAISY FAIRY

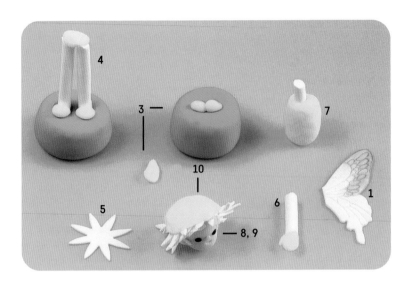

Materials:
- 20g (⅔oz) green
  modelling paste
- 5g (⅙oz) flesh-coloured fondant
  (sugarpaste)
- 5g (⅙oz) yellow
  modelling paste
- 5g (⅙oz) yellow
  fondant (sugarpaste)
- 10g (⅓oz) white modelling paste
  for the wings and daisy petals
- Five candy sticks
- Tiny amount of black fondant
  (sugarpaste) for the eyes
- Edible powder food
  colour green
- Thick edible glue

Tools:
- Large butterfly cutter
- Dusting brush
- Daisy flower cutter
- Non-stick rolling pin
- Small drinking straw
- Thin palette knife
- Plastic sandwich bag
- Water brush
- Dresden tool or cocktail stick
- Tissue paper

Instructions:

1 Roll out the white modelling paste and cut out a pair of butterfly wings with a large butterfly cutter. Gently brush green powder food colour over the surface. Leave to dry for a few hours or overnight.

2 For the base, shape the green modelling paste to a drum shape.

3 For the shoes, make two small pea-sized pieces of yellow fondant (sugarpaste) and shape each to an oval. Attach to the top of the drum.

4 For the legs, push two candy sticks straight down through one end of the shoes to the very bottom of the base. This will help support the standing figure. Attach a pea-sized piece of yellow fondant (sugarpaste) on top of the legs to form the base of the body.

5 Roll out white modelling paste thinly. Cut out two daisies, dampen the centres and stick them one on top of the other on the base of the body to make the skirt.

6 For the arms, cut two candy sticks to slightly shorter than the legs. For the hands, make two pea-sized pieces of yellow fondant (sugarpaste) to form simple hand shapes and cut out a tiny triangle from each to form thumbs. Dampen the ends of the arms and attach the hands.

7 Make an egg shape of yellow modelling paste for the body with a candy stick for support, slightly sticking out for the neck. Dampen the top ends of the arms and push them into the body. Cut out two more daisy flowers and stick them on to form a collar. Attach the body to the top of the legs. Leave to dry overnight, propped upright.

8 Make the head following step 7, page 39.

9 Cut out four more daisy flowers. Cut each flower into segments and stick to the head around the face.

10 Form a ball of yellow fondant (sugarpaste), just bigger than a pea. Flatten around the edge, widening it enough to cover the back of the head. Attach it. Texture the surface with a cocktail stick.

11 Attach the wings with thick edible glue, propping them up with scrunched-up tissue paper until dry.

12 Use thick edible glue to stick the head on top of the neck.

MALLARD

95

Materials:

- 10g (⅓oz) brown fondant (sugarpaste)
- Small amounts of grey, orange, green, white, black and blue fondant (sugarpaste)

Tools:

- Wing mould
- Dresden tool/cocktail stick

Instructions:

1 To make the body, form a 5cm (2in) long cone of brown fondant (sugarpaste).

2 For the wings, place a tiny piece of blue fondant (sugarpaste) at the tip of the wing feathers in the mould before putting in the grey fondant (sugarpaste). Stick the wings in place.

3 Take a small pea-sized ball of white fondant (sugarpaste) and flatten slightly to make the collar. Stick on to the body.

4 For the head, roll a large pea-sized ball of green fondant (sugarpaste) and stick it on top of the white collar. Attach tiny black eyes made from tiny balls of black fondant (sugarpaste).

5 To form the beak, roll a very small sausage of orange paste 1cm (³/₈in) long. Dampen the front of the face and lay the orange sausage vertically. Press the middle of the beak inwards, folding it in the middle. Gently curl up the end of the top beak and mark two tiny nostrils where the beak joins the face.

Simply Quackers!
To make a female mallard, mix brown and pale brown fondant (sugarpaste) together, and deliberately leave the colours mixed with blotches of colour.

CAKE KRAKEN

Materials:

20g (¾oz) red fondant (sugarpaste) or marzipan

2 edible black sugar pearls

Tools:

Zigzag wheel

No. 16 (4mm) piping tube

Instructions:

1 For the body, shape 10g (⅜oz) of fondant (sugarpaste) into an oval. Pinch the sides together at one end, and press that end gently to flatten it slightly.

2 Make two holes for the eyes and insert the black sugar pearls. Mark zigzag lines along the length of the body from behind the eyes.

3 Make two very tiny sausages for the eyelids and attach them over the eyes.

4 Make eight small pea-sized pieces, all the same size, and roll each one to a 15cm (6in) long pointed carrot for the legs. Emboss tentacles along each leg using the plain piping tube.

5 Shape each leg differently by twisting and curling.

6 Flatten and dampen the wide end of each leg. Attach the legs under the front end of the body.

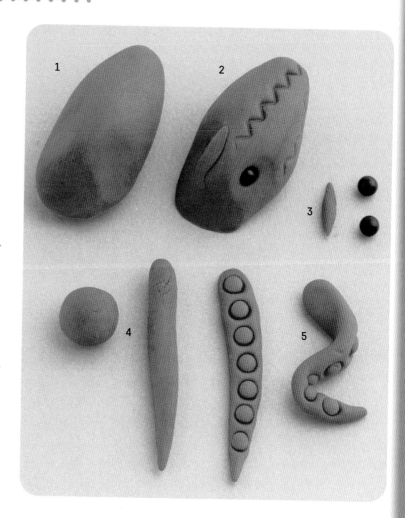

Beach Babe
Change the colours to suit the cake or celebration. You can also add more layers for a thicker, more stripy sole.

FLIP FLOPS

Materials:

Mexican (flower/gum) paste in white, purple and pink

Tools:

Small non-stick rolling pin

4cm (1½in) shoe sole cutter

2.5cm (1in) square cutter

Dresden tool

Multi-mould with tiny flower

Dogbone/ball tool

Small sharp pointed scissors

Waterbrush/small paintbrush and water

Instructions:

1 Roll out each of the coloured pastes to a thickness of 1mm (½oin). Cut out the 4cm (1½in) soles. Stick them carefully one on top of the other, dampening if necessary.

2 Roll out the white paste thinly. Allow to dry slightly on each side until the paste feels leathery. Cut out the 2.5cm (1in) square. Move the cutter slightly to cut the V-shape.

3 Use the Dresden tool to make a small hole on the top of the sole where the toe post would go. Dampen the hole. Dampen the sides of the sole where the straps will attach.

4 Lay the V-shape on the sole with the point over the hole. Press the point in with the Dresden tool. Flip the straps over and stick them to the sides. Cut through the excess with sharp pointed scissors.

5 For the flower, press a very tiny piece of white paste into the flower mould for the textured centre. Press a tiny piece of the purple paste into the mould on top of the white, using the dogbone/ball tool. The paste should only just come up to the surface of the mould. Take the flower out of the mould straight away, dampen the back and stick it on to the centre of the straps.

On Your Marks
Looking tense on their starting blocks these two athletes prepare for their sprint. Make a running track like this one out of colourful sprinkles and liquorice strands.

RUNNING

Instructions:

1 For the legs, roll one circle of brown paste into a long sausage shape measuring 11.5cm (4½in) long and cut it in half.

2 Bend each leg in half and pinch at the knee between your finger and thumb to define the knee joint. Secure both legs together at the top with a little sugar glue.

3 For each shoe, roll an eighth of a black paste circle into an oval, flatten slightly and run a cutting wheel around its edge to look like a sole. Secure under each leg with sugar glue and leave to dry overnight.

4 For the shorts, take one circle of white paste and roll it into an oval shape, then a rectangle with rounded edges. Hollow out the bottom end of the shorts slightly with the ball tool (for the legs) and mark on the central line with the leaf veining tool. Bend into the runner's starting position.

5 For the vest, take one and a half circles of white paste and roll into an oval shape. Push your thumb up into the base to hollow it out slightly and make each shoulder strap by pinching the paste on each side at the top between a finger and thumb. Attach it on to the shorts and bend at the waist to pose the figure. Push a popsicle stick into the vest to help keep the head from falling off. Secure the vest onto the shorts with sugar glue.

6 Using the blue edible ink pen, add a stripe detail down each side of the shorts when they are dry.

7 For the chest, take an eighth of a circle of brown paste and roll it into a ball, then into a triangular shape with rounded edges. Ease it into the top of the vest and pinch away any excess paste.

8 For the head, take a circle of brown paste and follow step 8, page 49. For the ears and nose, follow steps 10 and 11, page 49 and draw on the eyes and eyebrows with the black edible ink pen. Use a mini scallop tool for the mouth. To make the hair, roll three very small teardrops of black paste between your fingers and secure them to the top of the head with sugar glue.

9 To make the arms, take one circle of brown paste and model following step 6, page 49. Pinch each arm at the elbow between your finger and thumb to define the joint and leave the hands mitten-shaped. Attach to either side of the vest at the straps.

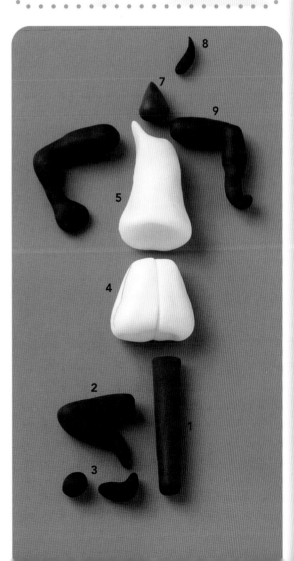

SCOTTIE DOG

Materials:

- 25g (just under 1oz) black modelling paste
- Very small piece of red modelling paste
- Edible candy stick
- Edible black sugar pearls
- Clear piping gel (optional)

Tools:

- Small petal cutter
- Dresden tool
- Dusting brush
- Water brush
- Thin palette knife
- Tea strainer/small sieve
- Multi-mould (tiny bow)
- Small non-stick rolling pin

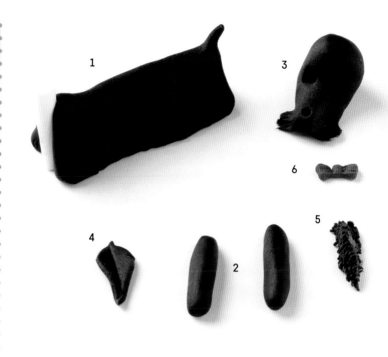

Instructions:

1 Shape 15g (½oz) of black paste to a 5cm (2in) sausage for the body. Flatten the sides to form a long triangle. Pinch and shape a small tail. Mark long fur with the Dresden tool. Attach an edible candy stick at the front end for the neck.

2 Shape two small pea-sized pieces of black paste to sausages the same height as the body. Dampen and press them into place to hide the candy stick support. Mark long fur with the Dresden tool.

3 Shape 2.5g (¹⁄₁₀oz) paste to a long pear shape for the head. Turn up the narrow end slightly for the nose. Pinch and shape the sides of the muzzle to make them hang down more. Use the Dresden tool to texture the muzzle. Shape the fat end of the head gently to form a higher forehead. Mark the eyes and nose with a Dresden tool and insert edible black sugar pearls. Dampen the top of the neck and press the head into place.

4 Roll out the paste thinly and cut out two small petal shapes for the ears. Attach them to the back of the head with the points upwards.

5 Dampen the eyebrows where the fluff will go. Push black paste through the tea strainer or sieve to make fluff. When you have the length you want, cut it off with a knife and attach it to form the eyebrows. Press into place with a Dresden tool as your fingers may flatten the fluff. If you have trouble getting it to stay on, use clear piping gel as a glue instead of dampening with water.

6 Make a tiny bow by pressing red modelling paste into the tiny bow mould. Dampen and attach to the neck.

CHRISTMAS ELF

Materials:

55g (2oz) dark green modelling paste

30g (1oz) flesh-coloured modelling paste

Small amounts of red, brown, yellow and black modelling paste

Small amount of white flower paste

One red and white striped chenille stick

Pale pink, brown and silver dusting powders

Cocktail stick

Tools:

Cutters: large star, small circle, large oval 6cm (2⅜in)

Fine black fibre-tip pen

Sieve

Sugar glue

Tool-shaped sugarcraft cutters and moulds

Jim
So many toys to make, so little time ... The little toy soldier is made from spare red, black and flesh-coloured paste, with a little gold dusting powder for the buttons.

10

11

8

9

7

12

3

6

13

4

5

Instructions:

1 Make a basic body in green as shown on page 20, insert an 8cm (3¼in) cocktail stick and make two holes in the front for the legs with a pointed tool.

2 For the head, roll 20g (⅔oz) of flesh-coloured paste into a smooth ball. Use a pointed tool to make a hole in the middle of the face for the nose and use the smiley tool to mark the mouth. Leave to dry.

3 Cut out a large oval from red paste to make the waistcoat. Attach the oval to the top of the body at the back with a little glue, bringing the thin ends of the oval to the front.

4 Cut two 7.5cm (3in) lengths from the chenille stick. For the shoes, cut a 15g (½oz) ball of black paste in half to make two flat ovals. Lightly glue both ends of one of the lengths of chenille stick, then insert one end into the top of the shoe and the other end into the body. Repeat with the other leg.

5 Cut a 2g (¹⁄₁₂oz) ball of red paste in half and roll into two smaller balls. Lightly glue one to the top of each shoe. Allow to dry, then bend each leg into shape.

6 To make the hands, cut a 3g (⅛oz) ball of flesh-coloured paste in half to make two flat ovals. Attach the hands to each end of the remaining 15cm (6in) length of chenille stick with sugar glue. Bend the chenille stick around the back of the cocktail stick and glue in place, bringing the arms and hands down.

7 Roll out the yellow paste and cut out two large stars. Using a little sugar glue, place a star on top of the chenille stick. Repeat with a second star, then glue the head on firmly.

8 For the ears, cut a 3g (⅛oz) ball of flesh-coloured paste in half, then roll each half into a smaller ball. Insert the rounded end of the pointed tool into one of the balls and, keeping the tool in place, pinch the top of the paste to make the ear pointed. Lightly glue the back of the ear and push it on to the side of the head. Repeat with the other ear. When dry, mark the eyes with the fine black fibre-tip pen and dust the cheeks with the pale pink dusting powder.

9 Roll out the brown paste for the hair. Cut out several circles with the small circle cutter. Cut into the edge of each circle halfway round and carefully open the strands out. Glue each piece individually on to the head. Work all the way round the head with two rows. The hole in the middle will be covered by the hat.

10 For the hat, roll out 10g (⅓oz) of dark green paste into a ball. Make the ball into a cone by opening out the middle with a large pointed tool and stretching the top to a point as shown, bending it over to the side. Glue the hat on to the top of the head.

11 To make the bobble, push a small piece of yellow paste though a sieve. Attach it to the top of the hat with a little glue.

12 Roll out a small circle of black paste and glue it to the middle of the waistcoat as a button.

13 Make the tools from white flower paste using the sugarcraft cutters and moulds. Colour them with brown and silver dusting powders and glue one to the hand, as shown.

TIGER

Instructions:

1 Divide the orange paste, taking about 20g (²⁄₃oz) for the body. Make a long, pointed oval. Cut into the ends to make the legs. Smooth the cut edges. Mark the toes with a cocktail stick. Push in a short candy stick (not shown) at the top of the front legs to support the head. Divide the rest of the paste into a large pea size for the tail, and what is left for the head.

2 Make the tail from a long sausage with a black piece rolled into the end.

3 Make a ball for the head.

4 Make stripes from black fondant (sugarpaste) by rolling very thin, pointed sausages 2cm (¾in) long. Stick them across the body, legs, tail and head. Attach the tail to the body.

5 To make the face, cut out a black heart with the heart cutter and flatten the edge slightly to widen it. Cut out a white heart and press on top of the black one, so the edge of the black shows. Stick on to the head.

6 Attach two small white ovals for the cheeks, a small black triangle for the nose, and two tiny black eyes. Use a cocktail stick to mark whiskers in the cheeks.

7 Stick the head on to the body at the top of the front legs.

8 For the ears, make two small balls of black and two smaller balls of white. Press the white gently on to the black.

9 Make two small sausages of white and flatten along the edges. Join the fat edge down the sides of the head. Make snips along the edges using the scissors to make them look fluffy.

10 To make the back paws, make two small balls of pink. On each one, press three tiny pink balls for the toes. Stick into place.

Materials:

35g (1¼oz) orange fondant (sugarpaste)

Small pieces of black, white and pink fondant (sugarpaste)

Candy stick

Tools:

Fine palette knife

Cocktail stick

Heart cutter, 2.5cm (1in)

Sharp pointed scissors

109

DANCING GROOM

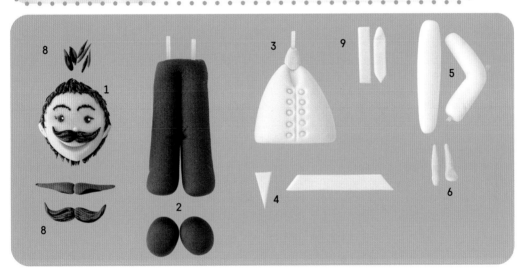

Materials:

Modelling paste: flesh-coloured: 12g (½oz);
brown: pinhead-sized piece; dark grey: 23g (⅘oz); light
blue: 21g (¾oz); white: 7g (¼oz); dark brown and black
mixture: 5g (⅙oz)

Sugar/spaghetti sticks

Edible glue/pasteurised egg white

White and black gel food colouring

Tools:

Cutting mat

Non-stick rolling pin

Scalpel/craft knife

Small paintbrush

Piping nozzle (tube)

Dresden tool/skewer

Instructions:

1 Using brown paste for the eyes, make a cone-shaped head from 10g (⅓oz) of flesh-coloured paste, and features as described in steps 1–5, page 31.

2 Make the trousers from 20g (⅔oz) of dark grey paste and the shoes from 3g (¹⁄₁₀oz) of dark grey paste, following steps 2 and 3 on page 59.

3 Make a waistcoat from the light blue paste follow the instructions for the jacket in step 4, page 59.

4 Make the neck using a pea-sized piece of flesh-coloured paste and the shirt and collar using a pea-sized piece of white paste, following step 5 on page 59.

5 Roll 10g (⅓oz) of white paste into two sausages to make arms. Bend each arm slightly in the middle and

attach the sleeves towards the front of the body. Push a sugar stick/spaghetti into the end of each arm and into the body. Leave to dry overnight.

6 Make the hands following step 9 on page 59.

7 Attach the head to the neck and turn it slightly sideways. Allow to dry overnight.

8 Make the hair and moustache with dark brown and black paste mixture, using thin tapered suasages for the hair and two short thick elongated cones for the moustache. Attach with edible glue/egg white.

9 Make a tie from a pea-sized piece of light blue paste following step 12 on page 59.

PINK ROSE BAG

Materials:

- Mexican (flower/gum) paste in bright pink
- Pearl white edible powder food colour
- A little alcohol for painting

Tools:

- Small, non-stick rolling pin
- Garrett frill cutter
- Petal veiner tool
- 6cm (2⅜in) and 2.5cm (1in) circle cutters
- Dresden tool
- No. 2 or 3 piping tube
- Cocktail stick
- Cutting wheel/sharp knife
- Music stave cutter
- Large stitching wheel
- Small sharp pointed scissors
- Waterbrush/fine paintbrush
- Plastic sandwich bag

Instructions:

1 Roll out the paste thinly. Allow it to dry slightly on each side until it feels leathery. Cut out a frilled circle with the Garrett frill cutter, the straps using the music stave cutter, one 2.5cm (1in) circle, a strip of paste 1 x 8.5cm (⅜ x 3⅜in), and a very tiny thin strip for the stay on the strap.

2 Cut the middle out of the frilled circle using the 6cm (2⅜in) circle. Cover the other pieces with the plastic sandwich bag to keep soft until required.

3 Further frill around the Garrett frill by rolling the edge firmly with the petal veiner tool.

4 Dampen around the inside (flat edge) and fold the frill on to itself to make a double layer frill. Dampen along the flat edge of the double frill and carefully roll up to make a rose.

5 Curve the petals outwards and tweak to make a rose shape. Make sure that the edges of the petals will make the rose slightly bigger than the 2.5cm (1in) base of the bag.

6 Roll the large stitching wheel down the middle of the wider strip of paste twice to make a stitching pattern to look like a zip. Paint the zip with pearl white edible powder mixed with a little alcohol, using the fine paintbrush.

7 Turn the strip over; dampen along one long side edge. Wrap it around the 2.5cm (1in) circle. Dampen where the strip overlaps to join it.

8 Mark two of the music stave cutter strips with a piping tube at one end.

Attach one of the straps to the circle bag. Cut the remaining strap to a point at the other end and mark tiny holes with a cocktail stick. Attach the strap to the bag. Join the straps by overlapping. Attach the tiny thin strip around the straps. Paint that thin strip and the two tiny circle marks with the pearl white edible powder mixed with a little alcohol.

9 Dampen the centre of the bag and attach the rose in the centre.

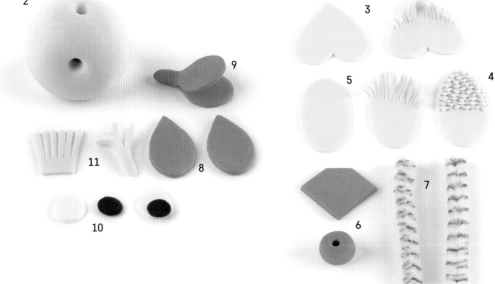

2

9

11

8

10

3

5

4

7

6

CHICK

Materials:

100g (3½oz) yellow modelling paste

Small amounts of orange, white and black modelling paste

One yellow or orange chenille stick

Cocktail stick

Tools:

Cutters: various size oval, small round, small square, very small petal, heart

Thin palette knife

Small pair of scissors

Sugar glue

Rolling pin

Instructions:

1 Make a basic body in yellow as shown on page 20, insert an 8cm (3¼in) cocktail stick, then make two holes in the front for the legs with the pointed tool.

2 Roll 20g (¾oz) of yellow paste into a ball for the head and shape as shown. Using a pointed tool, make a hole in the middle of the face for the beak and one at the top of the head for the feathers. Attach the head to the body with a little glue.

3 Roll out the yellow paste and use the heart cutter to cut one heart shape as the basis for the tail. Snip the top with scissors as shown, then use sugar glue to attach it to the back of the body with the round ends tucked under the base. Fluff out the tail to look like feathers.

4 Using yellow paste and the oval cutter, cut out one large oval for the tummy. Use the scissors to cut into the paste as shown, then lightly glue it and attach to the front of the body.

5 Cut out another two large ovals of yellow paste for the wings. Snip the narrow end of one and attach the other end of it to the back of the body with sugar glue before bringing it forward as shown. Repeat to make the second wing.

6 Use the small square cutter to cut out two small squares from the orange paste to form the basis for the feet. Cut off one small corner from each with scissors. Roll 5g (⅙oz) of orange paste into a ball then cut it in two. Roll each half into a ball and place one on top of each foot using a little sugar glue.

7 Cut two 7cm (2¾in) lengths of chenille stick, and add sugar glue to each end. Attach a foot to one end and insert the other end into the body. Repeat with the other leg and foot.

8 Make the parts for a beak by rolling out the orange paste and cutting out two small petal shapes with the petal cutter.

9 Join the parts of the beak together with a little glue at the pointed end and push them into the hole at the front of the head using the pointed tool.

10 For the eyes, use cutters to cut out two small ovals of white paste and two very small circles of black paste. Using a little glue attach the white ovals on the face just above the beak, then glue the black circles on top, as shown opposite.

11 Roll out a small thin strip of yellow paste, snip with scissors and roll up as shown. With a pointed tool, push the feathers into the top of the head using a little glue.

Kaz
The baby chick on the right (opposite) is made in the same way as Kaz, only half the size. The eyes are two small black dots added using a black fibre-tip pen.

Summer Fun
Gerberas are bright and bold flowers that look great on wedding cakes and as a trendy finish for cupcakes.

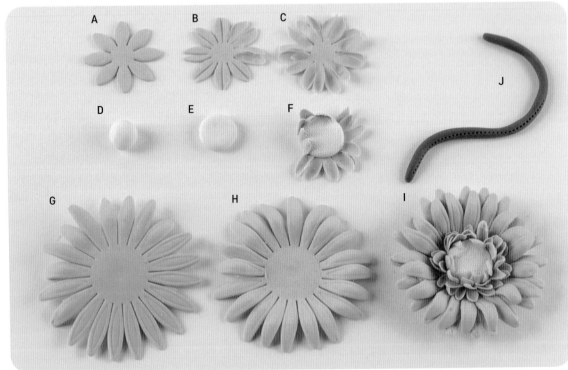

A

B

C

D

E

F

J

G

H

I

GERBERA

Materials:

Mexican (flower/gum) paste in pink, yellow and green
Powdered food colour in yellow, green and pink
Royal icing: white

Tools:

Sunflower/gerbera plunger cutter: 70mm (2¾in)
Daisy marguerite plunger cutter: 30mm (1¼in) and 27mm (1in)
Ivy leaf plunger cutters: 43mm (1¾in), 28mm (1⅛in)

Mini quilting tool
Flower former
Round plaque cutter: 100mm (4in)
Mexican foam balling pad
Sieve
Paintbrush: 12mm (½in) flat
Mini modelling tool
Ball tool

Instructions:

1 Cut out a daisy shape using the 27mm (1¼in) daisy marguerite cutter (A).

2 Use a craft knife to make a central cut along each petal to divide it into two (B).

3 Place a mini modelling tool vertically on the petal, with the tip of the tool at the centre of the flower. Roll the tool from side to side to widen and thin the petals. Place the piece on to a Mexican foam modelling pad and pull the ball tool from the tip to the base of the petals to cup them (C). Ensure you use cornflour on your board and tool to stop the paste from sticking.

4 Roll a pea-sized ball of yellow paste (D).

5 Push the ball of yellow paste against the surface of the sieve to flatten it into a textured disc (E).

6 Paint the centre of the medium prepared daisy shape with sugar glue and stick the yellow textured disc into the centre. Wrap the petals up around the sides of the disc (F). Use a little extra sugar glue to secure if needed.

7 Prepare two more sets of petals repeating steps 1–3 above (G and H), this time using the slightly larger 30mm (1¼in) cutter. With sugar glue, stick these two sets of petals one on top of the other so that the petals interleave, then stick the prepared yellow centre into the centre of the petals (I).

8 On a non-stick surface, roll out some pink paste quite thinly. Cut a large daisy shape out of the paste using the sunflower/gerbera plunger cutter (G).

9 Place the flower on the foam balling pad, then rub a ball softly around the tips of each petal to soften and shape. Flip the flower over and pull the ball tool from tip to base of petals to cup slightly (H).

10 Prepare a second flower in the same way. With a little sugar glue, stick the two large flowers together, placing one on top of the other and positioning the petals of the second layer so that they fall over the gaps in between the petals of the previous layer. Stick the prepared yellow centre into the middle of the flower with sugar glue and then place it in a flower former to dry.

11 Once dry, use the flat brush to dust the edges of the petals with some dark pink powdered food colour.

12 To assemble, roll a thin sausage of green paste to make a stem and stick on to a prepared round plaque sprayed with pearl lustre colour. Run a mini quilting tool along the stem to stitch (J).

13 Prepare several unwired ivy leaves by cutting small ivy leaf shapes from green paste. Place the leaves on top of a rolled-out piece of cream paste. With a small rolling pin, roll over the surface of the paste to merge the green ivy leaf shape into the cream paste. Take the larger ivy leaf plunger cutter and cut out and vein the leaf.

14 Stick these and the gerbera on to the plaque, using a little royal icing, to finish.

Shall We Dance?
This beautiful fairy and her friend in white and yellow would make lovely cake toppers for a birthday girl who loves dancing.

DANCING FAIRY

Materials:

10g (¾oz) flesh-coloured fondant (sugarpaste)

Pink fondant (sugarpaste):
10g (⅓oz) for the body, 10g (⅓oz) for the skirt, hands, feet and hair

10g (⅓oz) white modelling paste for the wings

Five candy sticks

Tiny amount of black fondant (sugarpaste) for the eyes

Thick edible glue

Tools:

Small butterfly cutter

Carnation cutter

Tiny blossom cutter

Non-stick rolling pin

Small drinking straw

Thin palette knife

Plastic sandwich bag

Water brush

Dresden tool or cocktail stick

Tissue paper

Instructions:

1 Roll out the white modelling paste and cut it with a small butterfly cutter. Leave to dry for a few hours.

2 Make the legs from two candy sticks. For the shoes, make two pea-sized pieces of pink fondant (sugarpaste) and shape each to a point. Dampen the ends of the legs and attach the shoes. Make a pea-sized piece of fondant (sugarpaste) to stick the top ends of the legs together, end to end.

3 For the tutu, roll out thin pink fondant (sugarpaste). Cut out at least three carnation flowers. Frill the edges with a cocktail stick. Dampen the middle of each and stick one on top of the other on the top of the legs.

4 Make an egg shape of pink fondant (sugarpaste) for the body with a candy stick for support, slightly sticking out. Dampen the bottom of the body and stick on top of the tutu.

5 For the arms, cut two candy sticks a little shorter than the legs. For the hands, make two pea-sized pieces of pink fondant (sugarpaste) to form simple hand shapes, then cut out a triangle from each to form thumbs. Dampen the ends of the arms and

attach the hands. Stick the arms into the body.

6 Make the head following step 7, page 39.

7 For the hair, roll out a piece of pink pea-sized fondant (sugarpaste) to cover the back of the head. Dampen and stick it in place. Mark it with a knife to look like hair. Attach a small ball of fondant (sugarpaste) for a bun.

8 Dampen the end of the neck and attach the head.

9 Attach the wings with thick edible glue.

10 Cut out two tiny blossoms from white modelling paste and stick them on the shoes.

11 Make very thin strands of pink fondant (sugarpaste) and twirl them into coils around a cocktail stick. Dampen the front edge of the hair, and stick the twirls of paste around the edge of the face.

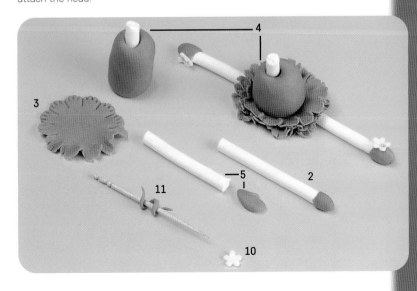

To make a more festive feathered friend, mark a line down the centre of the red heart, then mark on buttons with the piping tube. Make a cone of red paste and hollow the fat end slightly with your finger and thumb. Attach it to the top of the head and bend the point over to one side. Make white 'fluff' by pushing small amounts of fondant (sugarpaste) through a sieve/sugarcraft gun. Attach the 'fluff' around the base of the hat, and on the point of the hat to make a bobble (see above, right).

ROBIN

Materials:

25g (just under 1oz) brown or chocolate
   fondant (sugarpaste)

Small amounts of red, white and black
   fondant (sugarpaste)

Tools:

Heart cutter: 2.5cm (1in)

Dresden tool/cocktail stick

No. 2 piping tube

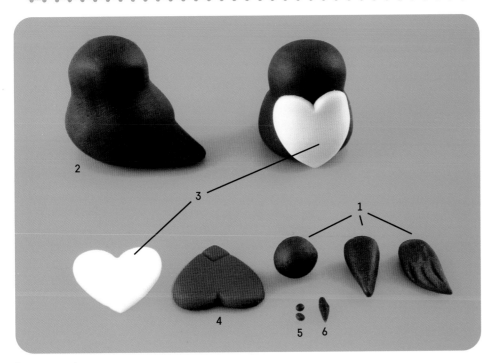

Instructions:

1 Make two wings from two small pea-sized pieces of the brown fondant (sugarpaste) rolled into cones. Mark with the Dresden tool for the feathers.

2 For the body, shape a pointed cone, 6cm (2½in) long, from brown fondant (sugarpaste). Roll the wide end gently between your two fingers to form a short, fat neck. Stand the model up by bending the tail back. Mark the feathers on the tail with the Dresden tool.

3 Cut out a white heart from some rolled-out white paste. Attach it to the body, point down.

4 Cut out a red heart from some rolled-out red paste. Cut the pointed end off with the pointed end of the heart cutter. Attach it upside down, above the white heart, overlapping.

5 Push the piping tube into the red heart on the head to form eye sockets. Make tiny eyes from balls of black fondant (sugarpaste) and stick them into the eye sockets.

6 Make a tiny pointed beak from black fondant (sugarpaste) and stick it in place.

7 Attach the wings.

MEAN MERLIN

Materials:

50g (1¾oz) purple modelling paste

Small piece of flesh-coloured fondant (sugarpaste) for the face

Small piece of white fondant (sugarpaste) for the beard, moustache and eyebrows

Clear piping gel

Tiny edible stars

Tools:

Food-grade kebab stick, barbecue stick or cake-pop stick

Rolling pin

1.5cm (½in) circle cutter

Cocktail stick or toothpick

Dresden tool

2.5cm (1in) square cutter

Small nylon-mesh tea strainer or sieve

Small, fine palette knife

Instructions:

1 Shape 25g (1oz) of purple modelling paste into a 10cm (4in) long pointed carrot. Push the stick into the fat end as far as possible without it coming out at the top.

2 Roll out the flesh-coloured fondant (sugarpaste) thinly and cut out a 1.5cm (½in) circle. Attach the circle to the purple body as shown. Mark a small hole in the centre for the nose, and press the Dresden tool in for the eyes. Make sure you push through to the purple layer to make the eyes dark.

3 Roll out the purple modelling paste and cut out two 2.5cm (1in) squares. Fold over each square diagonally to form triangles.

4 For each triangle, press one edge together and leave the other edge open for the sleeve. Dampen along the pressed edge and attach the sleeves to the sides of the body.

5 Press white fondant (sugarpaste) through the tea strainer or sieve for the beard. Cut the 'fluff' off in one piece if possible, using the small, fine palette knife. Dampen the body where the beard will go and attach it, pressing it into place with the cocktail stick or toothpick to avoid flattening it.

6 Make four tiny teardrop shapes from the white fondant (sugarpaste), and attach two for the moustache and two for the eyebrows.

7 Make a tiny nose from flesh-coloured fondant (sugarpaste). Stick it in place.

8 Dot piping gel over the pointed hat. Use a cocktail stick or toothpick dampened with a little of the piping gel to pick up tiny edible stars and attach them to the dots of gel on the hat.

BABY SNEAKERS

Materials:

Mexican (flower/gum) paste in white and dark blue

Tools:

Small non-stick rolling pin

5cm (2in), 3cm (1¼in) and 2cm (¾in) oval cutters

2.5cm (1in) circle cutter

Small fine palette knife

Cutting wheel

Waterbrush/small paintbrush
and water

Dogbone/ball tool

Quilting tool

Small sharp pointed scissors

Music stave cutter

Tiny star cutter

Instructions:

1 For the sole, roll out the white paste to 2mm (¹⁄₁₀in) thick. Cut out a 3cm (1¼in) oval.

2 Roll out blue paste thinly. Cut out a 2.5cm (1in) circle and a 5cm (2in) oval. Use a dogbone/ball tool to cup one end of the circle. Dampen around the side edge of the sole. Attach the front of the sneaker at the toe end. The top needs to curve upwards.

3 Use the cutting wheel to cut off a strip of about 2mm (¹⁄₁₀in) from the long side of the oval and discard it.

4 Roll out the white paste thinly. Cut out a 2cm (¾in) oval. Emboss a stitch pattern with the quilting tool along one edge. Stick to the front of the sneaker for the toe.

5 Dampen along the straight edge of the blue cut oval made in step 3 and wrap it round the back of the sole, overlapping the front of the sneaker.

6 Cut strips of white paste using the music stave cutter. Dampen the bottom edge of the sneaker and wrap one of the strips round the base. Join it at the back and cut off the excess with sharp pointed scissors.

Catch the Wave

This surf dude is ready to ride those waves! With his tanned skin, golden hair, shades and shorts, he certainly looks the part! Perfect for a sporty sun-worshipper!

The sail template is shown half of actual size. Enlarge 200% on a photocopier.

WINDSURFING

Materials:

Pale blue fondant (sugarpaste), 250g (8oz)

Modelling paste: orange, pale brown, black, bright yellow

White buttercream/frosting

Rice paper

Red edible dust

Edible lustre spray in blue

Piping gel

Food colouring in blue

Lollipop sticks

Sugar glue

Tools:

Marzipan/plastic spacers, 1.3cm (½in) depth

Non-stick rolling pin

Oval/fluted oval cutter, 12.7cm (5in)

Circle cutter, 2.5cm (1in)

Square cutter, 4cm (1½in)

Craft knife

Scriber

Smoother

Mini scallop tool

Mini ball tool

Piping tubes no. 3 or 4, 17

Small paintbrush

Kitchen paper

Leaf veining tool

Cutting wheel

Instructions:

1 Roll out the pale blue fondant (sugarpaste) and cut out the surfboard using the 12.7cm (5in) oval cutter and the base using the 12.7cm (5in) fluted oval cutter. Spray the fluted oval base with edible lustre spray in blue. When it has dried, secure the surfboard to the base with a little buttercream. Using the template, cut out a sail from rice paper.

2 For the legs, cut out two circles of pale brown paste and roll them into a sausage shape, 16.5cm (6½in) long. Bend the sausage in half to form two legs and insert a lollipop stick up through each ankle, leaving a little of the stick exposed at the end.

3 Bend the sausage in half to form two legs and insert a lollipop stick up through each ankle, leaving a little of the stick exposed at the end.

4 For the body, take one circle of pale brown paste and roll it into an oval shape, and then to a slight point for the waist. Add detail to the chest using the flat end of a leaf veining tool and secure to the legs, using sugar glue. Use a lollipop stick for reinforcement if necessary.

5 To make the shorts, roll out some orange paste thinly and cut out two squares using the 4cm (1½in) cutter. Use the straight comb edge of the mini scallop tool to mark a design around the waistband on each square. Secure one square to the front of your model and the other to the back to make up the shorts. Trim away any excess paste and smooth with your finger to neaten.

6 For the arms, take one circle of pale brown paste and roll it into a long sausage shape about 9.5cm (3¾in) long and cut it in half. Shape as shown opposite. Point the thumb upwards and curl the fingers inwards on one hand. For the other arm, position it away from the body in a waving position or ready to hold the sail and secure the arms to the body with sugar glue. Use kitchen paper to support the arms in position while they dry.

7 For the head, use half of a circle of pale brown paste and follow step 8, page 49. Make sunglasses by rolling out a very small amount of black paste and cutting out two circles using a no. 17 piping tube. Remove the top edge of each circle with a cutting wheel and secure each one either side of the nose.

8 Mould a few small teardrop-shaped pieces of bright yellow paste for the hair and position these randomly on the head for movement. When the figure is dry, secure the sail to the blue board with buttercream, anchoring it at the edges with a little leftover paste to hold it as it dries. When it is dry, position your windsurfer on the board, press the lollipop sticks from his feet into the board, and secure with a little buttercream. Use kitchen paper to keep him upright until everything has dried thoroughly.

9 Add on some piping gel coloured blue with food colouring around the surfboard for waves.

YORKSHIRE TERRIER

Instructions:

1 Shape 15g (½oz) of cream paste into a ball for the body. Insert a dampened edible candy stick, and model to a flat-bottomed 4cm (1½in) cone as shown. Pinch and shape a tail at the base, and mark an indentation for the front legs using the Dresden tool. Texture with the same tool to create long fur. Thin the edge of the tail to look like fur.

2 Brush over the surface using grey and brown edible powder food colour.

3 Shape 5g (⅙oz) of paste to a short pear shape for the head. Turn up the narrow end slightly for the nose. Shape the fat end gently to form a higher forehead. Mark the eyes and nose with a Dresden tool. Insert edible black sugar pearls for the eyes and nose. Dampen the top of the neck and press the head into place, tilting backwards to look cute. For best results, leave the dog to dry overnight before adding the fur.

4 Shape lots of tiny 1–2cm (⅜–¾in) sausages of chestnut paste and keep them soft under plastic. Start placing them in the middle of the head and nose, so that the fur hangs down. Mark with a knife or Dresden tool to look like fur. Make sure that the eyes and nose can be seen.

5 Roll out chestnut paste thinly and cut out petals for ears. Mark lines for the fur. Attach to the back of the head, with the points upwards.

Materials:
- 15g (½oz) cream-coloured modelling paste
- 10g (⅓oz) chestnut modelling paste
- Edible candy stick
- Edible black sugar pearls
- Brown and grey edible powder food colour

Tools:
- Small petal cutter
- Dresden tool
- Dusting brush
- Water brush
- Thin palette knife
- Plastic food bag/airtight box
- Small non-stick rolling pin

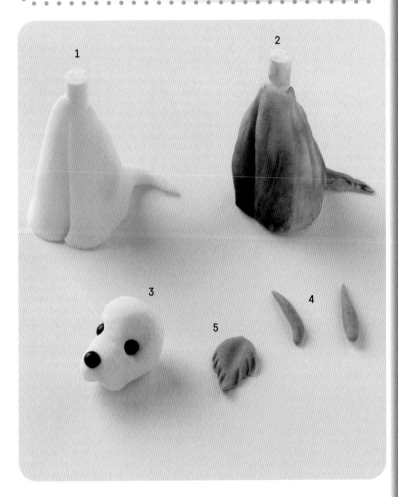

Anglia
A sugar mouse can hide from his beloved in a teacup if you make him slightly smaller!

MOUSE

Instructions:

1 Make a basic body in pink as shown on page 20 and insert an 8cm (3¼in) cocktail stick. Make two holes in the front for the legs.

2 Using a small amount of white paste, cut out an oval for the tummy, and glue in place.

3 Roll 20g (⅔oz) of pink paste into a smooth ball, then shape as shown for the head. Make holes for the eyes and nose. Insert two stamens for the eyes and mark the pupils using a black pen.

4 Roll a medium size ball of dark pink paste into a cone for the nose. Using glue, insert into the hole.

5 Cut a few bristles from the pastry brush and push them into the cheeks on each side of the face for the whiskers.

6 Mark the mouth with a circle cutter and use a pointed tool to make a hole at each end.

7 Use the circle cutters to cut out two pink outer ears and two white smaller inner ears. Do not roll the paste too thinly. Glue half a cocktail stick between the outer and inner ear and press down around the edges only. Push the assembled ears through the top of the head and leave to dry.

8 Cut a chenille stick in half and one piece in half again to make two 7.5cm (3in) legs and one 15cm (6in) arm.

9 To make the shoes, roll 16g (½oz) of pink paste into a ball and cut it in half to make two flat ovals. Use 10g (⅓oz) of paste to make the socks by rolling it into two small balls, making a hole in the top of each and then marking

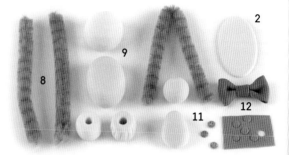

around the edges with a cocktail stick as shown. Secure one sock on top of each shoe with a little sugar glue.

10 Lightly glue one end of a 7.5cm (3in) pipe cleaner and insert into a sock and shoe. Lightly glue the other end of the pipe cleaner and insert into the body. Shape when dry. Repeat for the other leg.

11 For the hands, roll 6g (¼oz) of pink paste into a ball then cut it in half to make two ovals. Add sugar glue to each end of the 15cm (6in) pipe cleaner and attach the hands. Bend the pipe cleaner around the back of the cocktail stick, glue in place and bring the arms and hands down. Bend the arms into shape once the glue is dry.

12 Push the head on to the cocktail stick using a little sugar glue, then decorate with buttons and bows made from dark pink paste. Add a bunch of miniature flowers for a cute mouse.

SEAL

Materials:

20g (⅔oz) grey
   fondant (sugarpaste)
Small amount of black
   fondant (sugarpaste)

Tools:

Thin palette knife
Sharp pointed scissors
Drinking straw
Cocktail stick

Instructions:

1 To make the flippers, make two small cones and flatten slightly. Mark the wide end with a knife.

2 Roll the rest of the paste to form a long carrot shape.

3 Cut into the pointed end using the scissors to form the tail. Flatten it slightly. Roll the other end between your fingers to form a head. With the tail on the work surface, bend the body upwards.

4 Mark the lower part of the face with a drinking straw to form the cheeks, and add dots with a cocktail stick to look like whiskers. Mark the tail with a knife.

5 Attach the front flippers.

6 Stick on a small black triangle for the nose, and two small black eyes.

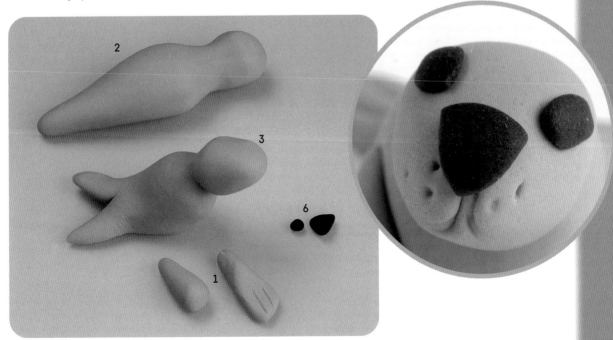

You can make a baby seal with white fondant (sugarpaste). This one is smaller than the adult and has a slightly simpler shape.

RUBY BRIDE

Materials:

Modelling paste: flesh-coloured: 13g
(½oz); black: 5g (⅙oz); brown: 5g
(⅙oz); maroon or red: 83g (3oz)
Sugar/spaghetti sticks
Edible glue/pasteurised egg white
White and black gel food colouring
Pink dusting powder

Tools:

Cutting mat
Non-stick rolling pin
Scalpel/craft knife
Piping nozzle (tube)
Small paintbrush
Toothpick
Dresden tool/skewer

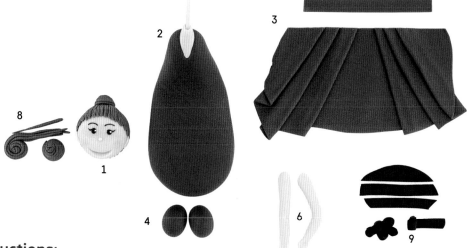

Instructions:

1 Make a round head, following steps 1–5, page 31, using black paste for the eyes.

2 Make a dress from 60g (2oz) maroon paste, following step 7, page 31. Bend the cone in half with the bottom of the dress pressed flat so that the bride will be in a seated position. Push a sugar/spaghetti stick into the bodice of the dress with 1.5cm (⅔in) protruding from the top.

3 Roll out 20g (⅔oz) of maroon paste until very thin. Cut a large rectangle, twice as wide as the bride. Pleat it, folding the pleats on each side towards the centre; cut off the top to

make it even. Drape it over the skirt of the dress from the back and attach it at the waist with edible glue. Tuck it in under her bottom and fold in the pleats at the seam of the dress. Cut a long rectangle and attach it to the waist.

4 Make shoes from 3g (⅒oz) of maroon paste following step 8, page 31; attach them to the bottom of the dress.

5 To make a neck follow step 9, page 31.

6 Make arms and hands following step 10, page 31. Place one arm next to the body hanging down and the other resting in the bride's lap.

7 Attach the head to the neck with edible glue.

8 Using brown paste, glue long tapered sausages to the head, placing each hair strand to reach from the forehead, ears and neck to the centre back of the head. Flatten the hair with your finger and mark it with a knife. Place long tapered sausages together and roll them up into a bun. Glue the bun to the centre back of the head.

9 Make tiny roses by rolling up thin strips of black paste, and attach to the hand in the bride's lap.

ZEBRA PRINT BAG

Materials:

- Mexican (flower/gum) paste in white and black
- 4mm (³⁄₁₆in) edible black sugar pearls
- Piping gel

Tools:

- Small, non-stick rolling pin
- 3cm (1¼in) oval cutter
- 6cm (2⅜in) circle cutter
- No. 2 or 3 piping tube
- Small, fine palette knife
- Cutting wheel
- Dresden tool
- Small sharp pointed scissors
- Waterbrush/fine paintbrush and water

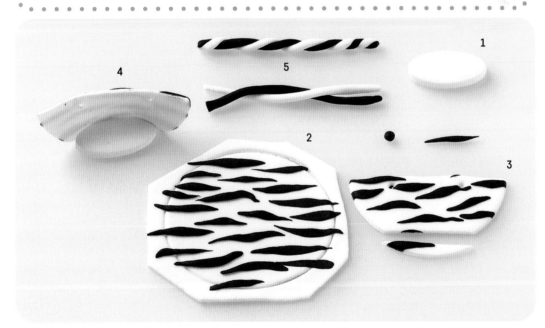

Instructions:

1 Roll out the white paste to around 3mm (⅛in) thick. Cut out the 3cm (1¼in) oval.

2 Roll out the white paste thinly. Mark with the 6cm (2⅜in) circle without cutting through. Use scissors to make lots of tiny black pointed pieces of paste as shown. Lay them over the white paste to form a zebra pattern and roll over with a rolling pin to fuse the colours together.

3 Cut the 6cm (2⅜in) circle. Use the cutting wheel to cut the circle in half, and cut a small piece 5mm off each end as shown. Use the piping tube to mark two holes in each side of the bag where the handles will be attached.

4 Dampen around the oval base and the inside, curved edge of the bag sides. Attach one side to the oval base, and then attach the other side to the first side, making sure that they line up.

5 To make the rope handles, roll pieces of white and black paste each to make a very thin sausage about 12cm (4¾in) long. Twirl the two colour pieces together, rolling to form a spiral. Cut to make two handles about 6cm (2⅜in) long. Dampen the inside marks on the bag and attach the handles.

6 Place a tiny dot of piping gel on the outer side where the handles join, and stick a black sugar pearl in place. Repeat at all the handle joining points. Prop the bag up to dry.

Charlie
Whatever colours you use for this cute little dinosaur's skin and dots, he will still look very fierce.

DINOSAUR

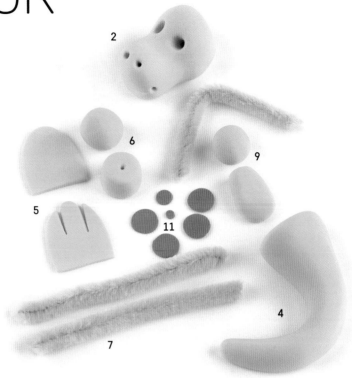

Materials:

120g (4¼oz) pale blue modelling
    paste

Small amount of orange Mexican
    (flower/gum) paste

Small amount of white paste

Two black stamens or
    two very small balls of
    black paste

One pale blue chenille stick

Cocktail stick

Instructions:

1 Make a basic body in pale blue as shown on page 20; make two holes at the front for the legs.

2 For the head, roll 23g (⅞oz) of pale blue paste into a ball and then shape as shown. Use the pointed tool to make two holes for the eyes and two holes for the nostrils, then use a large circle cutter to shape the mouth and make a small hole at each end with a pointed tool.

3 To make the eyes, shape two very small balls of white paste into tear drops and insert into the holes using a little sugar glue. Next, push in a black stamen or use very small balls of black paste.

4 Make the tail by rolling 24g (¹⁵⁄₁₆oz) of pale blue paste into a ball and rolling one end into a long tail. Push a cocktail stick half way into the back of the body at the base for extra support and push on the tail, using a little glue to secure it. Leave to dry.

5 Roll out two pale blue ovals for the feet and cut a small piece away from one end. Use the palette knife to make two cuts through the paste for the toes.

6 To make the ankles, roll two small balls of pale blue paste, flatten them slightly and glue them on to the feet.

7 Cut two 9cm (3½in) lengths of chenille stick for the legs and one 10cm (4in) length for the arms.

8 Lightly glue each end of a 9cm (3½in) chenille stick and insert one end into the foot and ankle and the other end into the body. Repeat for the second leg.

9 Roll 5g (⅙oz) of paste into a ball and cut it in half with the scissors to make two oval hands. Add a little sugar glue to each end of the 10cm (4in) chenille stick and attach the hands. Bend the chenille stick around the back of the cocktail stick, then glue it in place, bringing the arms and hands down.

10 Push the head on to the cocktail stick firmly using a little sugar glue. Leave to dry.

11 Cut out different size circles of orange paste for the spots, and attach them to the dinosaur with a little glue.

Fragrant Freesias
Always a popular choice for brides, these sugar flowers look great on their own or combined with other bridal flowers.

FREESIA

Materials:

- Mexican (flower/gum) paste in white
- Powdered food colour: yellow, burgundy, green

Tools:

- 28g wires: green (cut into quarter-lengths)
- Tiny dull round stamens: white
- Freesia cutter: 35mm (1⅜in)
- Paintbrushes: size 2/0 round, 12mm (½in) flat

Instructions:

Flowers

1 Make a Mexican hat by pinching the wide end of a cone of paste with your fingers and thumbs. This flattens and widens the base, leaving the pointed end of the cone as a stem standing up in the middle. Roll the flattened base area with a mini modelling tool to thin and widen even more, rolling from right up close to the stem to the outside edge (A).

2 Place the freesia cutter over the Mexican hat, push down and cut out the flower shape. Release from the cutter by pushing a ball tool into the centre of the flower. With a mini modelling tool, roll each petal vertically from side to side to widen, thin down and shape. Place on foam pad and soften the edges of the petals, then cup with a ball tool (B).

3 Roll out some white paste and cut out a freesia petal (C).

4 Prepare petals as described in step 2 (D).

5 Attach a thin piece of stem tape to the end of a 28g wire. Lay six stamens in place on the tape against the wire (E).

6 Bind the stamens to the end of the wire by winding the stem tape securely around them, continuing down the wire to the base (F).

7 With sugar glue, stick the flat petals on top of the Mexican hat petals, interleaving the petals. Brush a little sugar glue on to the wire at the base of the stamens. Insert wire and stamens into centre of the flower, secure by rolling paste at the back of the flower between fingers. With a small pair of scissors held at a 45-degree angle to the base of the stem, make a tiny cut into the paste on either side of the stem to create a small calyx (G).

8 Use the size 2/0 round brush to colour the centre of the white flowers with some yellow petal dust and leave the petals white. For the burgundy flowers, brush the outer edges of the petals from the stem upwards with some burgundy powdered food colour and a flat brush. Dust the calyx with green.

Buds

9 Insert a 28g wire into a large pea-sized ball of white paste (H).

10 Use your fingers to roll the paste at the base of the ball to thin it down and secure it to the wire (I).

11 Roll the top of the bud to taper slightly, then cut a calyx in place at the base of the flower with a pair of small scissors (J).

12 With fingers, push the top of the bud over to the side a little and mark lines with a pair of scissors (K).

13 To complete, colour the buds with some green powdered food colour using the flat brush. The smaller buds should be totally green and the larger buds should be green just at the base over the calyx. Dust the tips of the buds with the colour to match the flower.

14 Tape the buds and flowers together in a long stem using stem tape, starting with smallest buds and finishing with the flowers.

Little Sweethearts
Make the other baby in white fondant (sugarpaste), and dust the wings with edible pearl pink powder. These sweet babies would make a lovely gift to celebrate a new arrival, or cake toppers for a christening.

BABY FAIRY

Materials:

White fondant (sugarpaste);
  100g (3½oz) for the cloud and
  5g (⅙oz) for the hat

5g (⅙oz) white modelling paste
  for the wings

5g (⅙oz) flesh-coloured fondant
  (sugarpaste) for the head

15g (½oz) pale blue
  fondant (sugarpaste)

Candy stick

Tools:

Small butterfly cutter

Non-stick rolling pin

Small drinking straw

Thin palette knife

Plastic sandwich bag

Water brush

Dresden tool or cocktail stick

Tissue paper

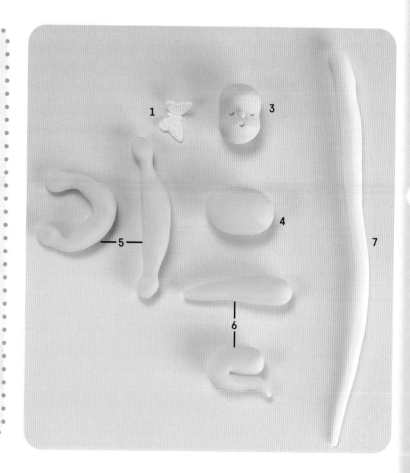

Instructions:

1 Roll out the white modelling paste and cut it with the small butterfly cutter.Leave to dry for a few hours or overnight.

2 Shape most of the white fondant (sugarpaste) to a simple cloud shape. Save a little for the hat.

3 To make the head follow step 7, page 39, but make closed eyes by pressing in the drinking straw, making a curve for each eye.

4 Divide the blue fondant (sugarpaste) into three equal parts. Use one to make an egg shape for the

body with a candy stick for support, slightly sticking out. Lay the body on the cloud, allowing space for the head to be added.

5 Make the second part into a sausage shape approximately twice the length of the head, and slightly thinner at each end for the hands. Flatten the hands slightly. Curve the arms forward and attach to the top of the body.

6 Divide the third piece of blue paste in two to make the legs. Roll each one to a carrot shape about twice the length of the body. Bend in half to

form a knee. Gently pinch to form the foot. Stick the legs in place.

7 Roll the remaining white fondant (sugarpaste) to a long carrot shape for the hat. Wind it around the head, starting with the fat end nearest the face, dampening if necessary, and pressing into place. Finish with a point on the back of the head.

8 Attach the wings with thick edible glue/gunge. Prop them up with scrunched-up tissue paper until the glue is dry.

PENGUIN

Instructions:

1 Roll out the black fondant (sugarpaste). Make a tiny ball of yellow fondant (sugarpaste) and press it on to the black. Cut out a black square with the cutter, cutting through the yellow on the corner of the square – this will form the beak. Mark on two eyes with the piping tube.

2 For the penguin's body, shape a cone from the white fondant (sugarpaste). The length needs to be shorter than the diagonal of the square. Stand the cone up on its base.

3 Cover the cone with the black fondant (sugarpaste) square with the yellow beak over the head first. The wings and tail can be left curved out or tweaked until the model resembles a penguin.

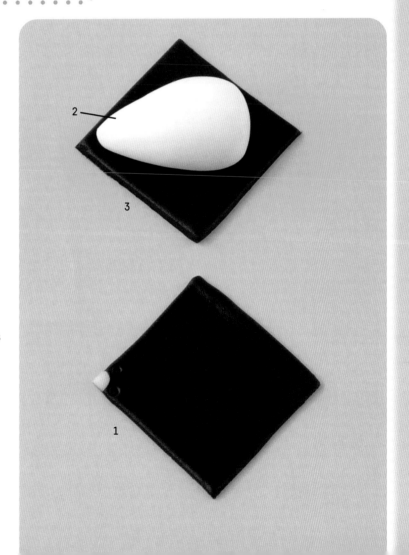

Easy as pie!
These sweet treats are as cool as ice, and a piece of cake to make!

The bat can be used flat on cakes straightaway or, if left to dry until hard, it could be stuck on the edge of a cake to look as if it is flying.

VAMPIRE BAT

Materials:

10g (⅜oz) black modelling paste

Tiny piece of white fondant
(sugarpaste) for the teeth

Tools:

Greaseproof paper or
    baking parchment

Wing template

Rolling pin

Dresden tool

Cutting wheel

Palette knife

Instructions:

1 Trace over and cut out a template for
the wings using greaseproof paper or
baking parchment.

2 Roll out black modelling paste thinly.
Cut around the wing template. Mark lines
for the wings as shown using a knife or
Dresden tool.

3 For the body, shape a small 2g (¹⁄₁₆oz)
pea of black modelling paste into a 2cm
(¾in) sausage. Shape the face forward to
a point.

4 Pinch the ears up from the sides of
the head.

5 Mark the eyes and nostrils with the
Dresden tool. Mark the mouth with a knife.

6 Roll out the white fondant (sugarpaste)
very thinly and cut out two tiny triangles
for the teeth. Stick them in place.

7 Alternatively, if you have any royal icing
or buttercream already made, pipe the
teeth on using a fine piping tube. You could
even paint the teeth on using white edible
food colour.

8 Stick the body to the wings.

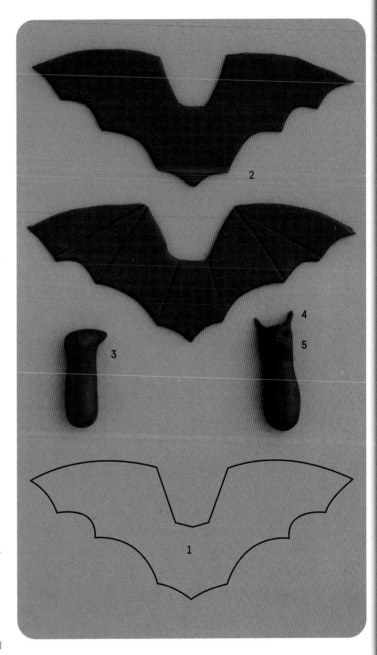

FOOTBALL BOOTS

Materials:

Mexican (flower/gum) paste in white and orange

Tiny silver balls

Piping gel/edible glue

Tools:

Small non-stick rolling pin

3cm (1¼in) shoe sole cutter

5cm (2in) and 2cm (¾in) oval cutters

1.5cm (⅝in) square cutter

Quilting tool

Small fine palette knife

Dresden tool

Small sharp pointed scissors

Waterbrush/small paintbrush and water

Instructions:

1 Roll out the white paste to a thickness of 1mm (¹⁄₂₀in). Cut out the 3cm (1¼in) sole. Make holes for the studs using the Dresden tool. Dot a tiny amount of piping gel or edible glue in each hole. Stick tiny silver balls into the holes and press them in gently. Allow to dry flat for at least 30 minutes, turning it over occasionally.

2 Roll out the orange paste thinly. Allow it to dry slightly on each side until the paste feels leathery. Cut out the 5cm (2in) oval and 1.5cm (⅝in) square. Use the 2cm (¾in) oval cutter to cut out the middle towards one end of the large oval and discard it. Cut straight across at the end as shown using the palette knife. Mark lines and dots

to represent the laces using the palette knife and Dresden tool. Mark small stitches using the quilting tool.

3 Dampen the sides of the sole. Attach the top to the sole starting at the toe end, gently pressing the paste carefully to the sides of the sole. Use the Dresden tool to help shape the boot from the inside. Dampen the ends and press them together. Cut through the excess with sharp pointed scissors.

4 Cut the 1.5cm (⅝in) square in half diagonally with the palette knife and mark stitching round the edge using the quilting tool. Dampen the underside and wrap around the back of the boot.

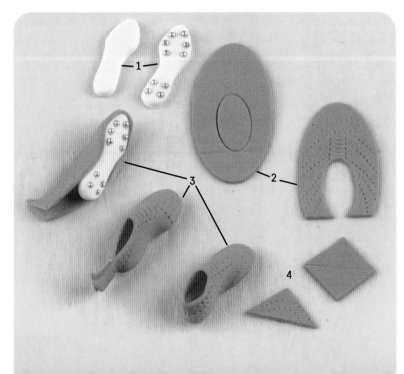

SAILING

Materials:

White fondant (sugarpaste), 340g (12oz)

Modelling paste: blue, white, orange, pale brown, yellow

Sugar glue

Rice paper

Edible ink pen in blue

Edible red dust

Tools:

Marzipan/plastic spacers, 1.3cm (½in) depth

Non-stick rolling pin

Circle cutter, 2.5cm (1in)

Oval cutter, 12.7cm (5in)

Square cutter, 4cm (1½in)

Cutting wheel

Leaf veining tool

Craft knife

Smoother

Scriber

Ball tool

Mini ball tool

Scissors

Ruler

Hole punch

Cookie stick

Small paintbrush

Piping tube no. 3 or 4

Sail Away

Use some edible lustre spray in blue on your rice paper sail to give it some movement – the spray makes it curl as if in the wind. Then your sailor's boat is ready to sail the sugary seas. For keen sailors, give your boat a name using an edible ink pen.

10

9

6

7

5

8

4

3

1

2

Instructions:

1 To make the boat, roll out some white fondant (sugarpaste) and cut out an oval using the 12.7cm (5in) cutter. Re-cut the shape to make it more of a boat shape with pointed ends using the cutter (see opposite).

2 Roll some white fondant (sugarpaste) into a sausage shape, flatten slightly to the depth of the spacers and add to the outside edge of the boat. Trim off any excess paste with a craft knife so that it fits the size of the boat, making sure the edges are neat. Use the cutting wheel to create a wood grain effect by dragging through the paste. Shape the front of the boat to more of a point than the back by smoothing the paste between your finger and thumb.

3 For the sail, use an edible ink pen to draw a triangle on to the sheet of rice paper measuring 10cm (4in) by 6.5cm (2½in) and cut out with some scissors. Use the hole punch to make two holes, one near the top and one near the bottom of the triangle. Thread the cookie stick through the holes, dip the end in sugar glue and push your sail into the inside of the boat towards the front.

4 For the legs, take two circles of blue paste, roll them into a ball and then make a sausage shape of paste measuring approximately 12.5cm (5in) long. Bend it in half, then bend one half (one leg) over the other and position at the side of the boat.

5 For the body, cut out one circle of blue paste, roll it into an oval shape and mark on the zip by using the sharp end of the leaf veining tool.

6 For the arms, use one circle of blue paste and roll it to a length of 6.5cm (2½in). Cut it in half, indent each end with the ball tool for the hands and add texture with a leaf veining tool. Cut across the top of each arm ready to attach them to the body.

7 For the life jacket, use the 4cm (1½in) square cutter and orange paste. Roll out the paste quite thinly and cut out one square using the same cutter. Cut this square in half using the cutting wheel or the square cutter. Remove a semi-circle from one side of each square using the 2.5cm (1in) circle cutter and discard. This shapes the paste into a vest with straps. Secure the life jacket to the body with sugar glue.

8 To make the hands, take a large pea-sized amount of pale brown modelling paste and shape as shown opposite. Secure them to the ends of the arms with sugar glue and secure one hand so that it rests on the edge of the boat and the other holding the sail.

9 Cut out half a circle of brown modelling paste to make the head and roll into a ball.Using a mini ball tool, approximately in the centre of the ball, make a recess for the nose. Push the tool lightly into the paste ball. To add colour to the cheeks, apply edible dust sparingly with a very small soft paintbrush; remove the excess on a piece of kitchen paper first. For the mouth, push a mini scallop tool into the paste to make a smile or frown and use a craft knife to add the corners of the mouth. For the nose, roll out some paste thinly and use no. 3 or 4 piping tubes to cut out a circle. Roll into a ball and secure into the recess in the centre of the head, using sugar glue. For the ears, roll out some paste thinly and use no. 3 or 4 piping tubes to cut out a circle. Roll it into a ball and cut it in half to make two ears. Attach one at each side of the head, using sugar glue Make the eyes following step 12, page 49. Secure the head to the body with sugar glue.

10 Create the hair by rolling small balls of yellow modelling paste into teardrop shapes. Secure them to the head, positioning them randomly, with sugar glue.

BICHON FRISE

Materials:

20g (⅔oz) white modelling paste

20g (⅔oz) white fondant (sugarpaste)

50g (1¾oz) red modelling paste

Edible candy stick

Edible black sugar pearls

Black food colour pen

Tools:

Small non-stick rolling pin

Petal veining tool

Small petal shape cutter

Dresden tool

Dusting brush

Water brush

Thin palette knife

Tea strainer/small sieve

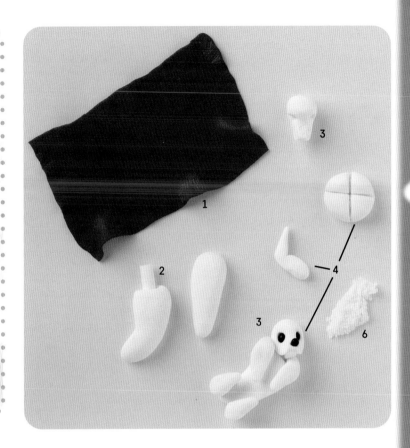

Instructions:

1 Roll out red paste thinly. Cut a blanket 8 x 6cm (3⅛ x 2⅜in). Frill the edge by rolling with a petal veining tool.

2 Shape 5g (⅙oz) of white modelling paste to a 4cm (1½in) cone for the body. Push in a short candy stick at the fat end for the neck as shown.

3 Shape 2.5g (¹⁄₁₀oz) of white modelling paste to a short pear shape for the head. Turn up the narrow end slightly for the nose. Shape the fat end gently to form a higher forehead. Mark the eyes and nose with a Dresden tool and insert edible black sugar pearls. Dampen the top of the neck and press the head into place.

4 Cut a 5g (⅙oz) piece of paste into four equal pieces for the legs. Roll each to form a 3cm (1¼in) sausage. Bend the front legs to form an 'L' shape and attach to the top of the body with the paws pointing away from the head.

Attach the back legs, bent in the same way, to the side of the body at the tail end, paws pointing to the head. Draw pads on the base of the back paws using the black food colour pen.

5 Lay the dog on the blanket.

6 Dampen the whole dog (except the feet on the back legs) where the fluff will go. Push the white sugarpaste through the tea strainer/small sieve to make fluff. When you have the length you want, cut it off with a knife and attach it to the dampened areas on the dog. Press into place with Dresden tool as your fingers may flatten the fluff. If you have trouble getting it to stay on, use piping gel as a glue instead of dampening with water. Make the ears and tail from the fluff, and stick it directly to the blanket. Make sure that the eyes and nose are visible.

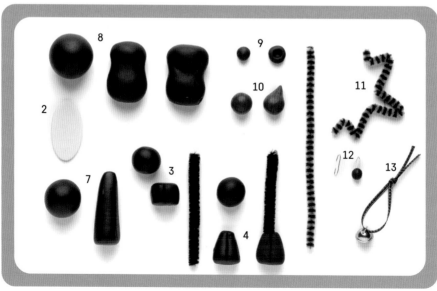

REINDEER

Materials:

110g (3¾oz) chocolate
   modelling paste

30g (1oz) black modelling paste

Small amount of cream, white and red
   modelling paste

Two brown chenille sticks

Small bell

Ribbon

Confectioners' glaze

Different coloured glitters

Fine wire

Two white stamens

Tools:

Tweezers

Cutter: 4cm (1½in) oval

Fine black fibre-tip pen

Sugar glue

Instructions:

1 Make a basic body using chocolate modelling paste, as shown on page 20, and use the pointed tool to make two holes in the front for the legs. Leave to dry.

2 Using the cream paste, cut out an oval for the tummy and glue in place on the front of the body.

3 For the hooves, roll out 30g (1oz) of black paste into a smooth ball and cut it into four pieces. Roll each quarter into a smaller ball. Roll two of the pieces into round flat discs and mark a line down the front of each disc.

4 Roll the other two balls of paste into truncated cones and mark a line down the front as shown.

5 Cut two 7.5cm (3in) lengths of chenille stick for the legs, add glue to both ends and insert one into the cone-shaped hoof and the other into the body. Repeat with the other cone-shaped hoof. Bend the legs into shape when dry.

6 Attach the round black disc-shaped hooves to the sides of the body, near the base, with a little glue.

7 For the arms, cut a 30g (1oz) ball of chocolate paste into two pieces, then roll each piece into a 5cm (2in) long cone shape. Attach the arm to the top of the hoof and the side of the body using a little glue, then smooth down the paste at the top of the body. Repeat with the other arm.

8 Make the head by rolling 30g (1oz) chocolate paste into a ball and then shaping as shown. Glue on to the top of the body. Using the pointed tool, make a hole in the top of the head for the antlers, two holes for the eyes and one for the nose. Insert the stamens for the eyes and use a fine black fibre-tip pen to mark the pupils. With a large circle cutter mark the mouth and use a pointed tool to mark the corners.

9 For the ears, cut a 2g (¹⁄₁₂oz) ball of chocolate paste in half and roll each piece into a smaller ball. Push the rounded end of a pointed tool into one ball. Glue the bottom part of the ear, and place it firmly on at the side of the head. Remove the tool and repeat with the other ear. Leave to dry.

10 Make a small cone of red paste for the nose and insert it into the hole with a little glue. When dry, paint with a little confectioners' glaze to make a shiny nose.

11 Fold a 15cm (6in) length of chenille stick in half for the antlers, then shape as shown opposite. Insert into the hole in the middle of the head.

12 For the glitterball decorations, roll out ten small balls of white paste and cut ten 2cm (¾in) lengths of wire. Make a small hook at each end of one of the pieces of wire then attach a small ball to one end with a little glue. Lightly cover the ball with glue and cover with glitter. Shake off the excess, and use tweezers to hook the other end of the wire over the chenille stick. Repeat with the other nine balls of paste using different coloured glitters.

13 Attach a bell to a small length of ribbon and tie around the back of the neck to finish off your reindeer.

The little koala is made in white with a lilac tummy, and seems to be waving a paw!

KOALA BEAR

Materials:

65g (2¼oz) lilac
  fondant (sugarpaste)
Small amounts of white and
  black fondant (sugarpaste)
Candy stick

Tools:

Drinking straw
Sharp pointed scissors
Thin palette knife
Heart cutter, 2.5cm (1in)

Instructions:

1 Divide the lilac fondant (sugarpaste), taking about 25g (just under 1oz) for the body, then form this into an egg shape and add a candy stick for support (not shown). Stick on a white heart shape for the tummy. Divide the rest of the lilac paste into four balls.

2 Take two of the balls and form each one into a carrot shape to make the legs. Mark toes with a knife. Attach the legs.

3 Divide one of the balls into two and make smaller carrot shapes for the arms. Mark the paws with a knife. Join the arms to the body.

4 The last lilac ball makes the head. Mark the mouth with a drinking straw. Attach the head to the body.

5 Make two small white ovals for the ears. Stick on the sides of the head, pushing in gently to cup them. Snip around the edges with scissors.

6 Make the nose from a black oval shape and the eyes from two tiny balls of black paste.

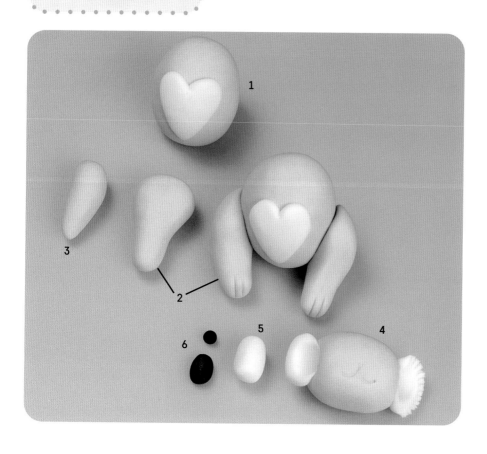

ROMANTIC GROOM

Materials:

Modelling paste: flesh-coloured: 12g (½oz);
    black: 63g (2¹⁄₁₀oz), brown: 5g (¹⁄₆oz);
    cream or ivory: pea-sized piece; peach:
    pea-sized piece

Sugar/spaghetti sticks

Edible glue/pasteurised egg white

White and black gel food colouring

Tools:

Cutting mat

Non-stick rolling pin

Scalpel/craft knife

Small paintbrush

Piping nozzle (tube)

Toothpick

Dresden tool/skewer

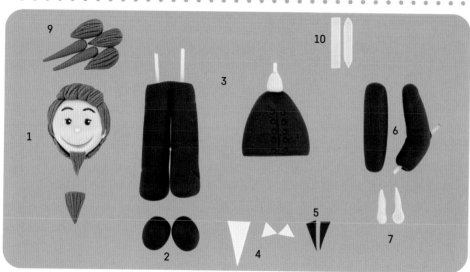

Instructions:

1 Make a head and face from 10g
(⅓oz) of flesh-coloured paste,
following steps 1–5, page 31, rolling
the head into a cone shape.

2 Make trousers from 20g (⅔oz)
of black paste and shoes from 3g
(¹⁄₁₀oz), following steps 2 and 3 on
page 59. Place one leg slightly in
front of the other.

3 Make the jacket from 20g (⅔oz) of
black paste, following step 4, page 59.

4 Make the neck using a pea-sized
piece of flesh-coloured paste, and the
shirt using a pea-sized piece of cream
or ivory paste, following steps 5 and
6, page 59.

5 Use 3g (¹⁄₁₀oz) of black paste to
make the jacket collar and lapels,
following step 7, page 59.

6 Make two sleeves from 10g (⅓oz)
of black paste, following step 8,
page 59. Bend each arm slightly in
the middle and attach the sleeves
towards the front of the body. Push a
sugar stick/spaghetti into the end of
each arm and into the body. Leave to
dry overnight.

7 Make and attach the hands,
following step 9, page 59.

8 Attach the head to the body and
leave to dry overnight.

9 Using brown paste to make gelled
hair and a goatee, glue thick medium-
sized tapered sausages onto the
head as shown. Place a few thick
medium-sized tapered sausages
on the forehead, gluing them from
the forehead towards the back of
the head, and mark the hair with a
knife. To make a goatee, roll a thick
medium-length tapered sausage
and flatten it with your finger. Mark
the paste with a knife and glue it to
the chin.

10 Make a tie with peach paste,
following step 12, page 59.

Make an alternative in red. These bright bags look perfect for the beach or summer shopping.

GEL BAG

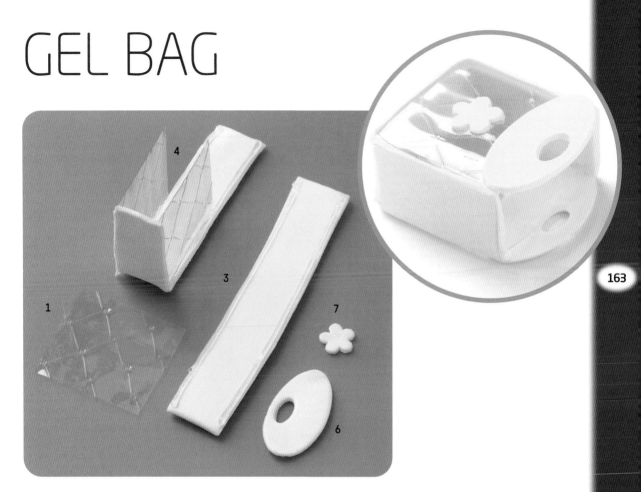

Materials:

Mexican (flower/gum) paste in yellow

Leaf gelatine sheets

Piping gel

Tools:

Small, non-stick rolling pin

Cutting wheel

Ruler

4cm (1½in) and 1cm (⅜in) oval cutters

Tiny blossom cutter

Small, sharp pointed scissors

Instructions:

1 Cut the gelatine sheets to make two 4cm (1½in) squares using the scissors.

2 Roll the yellow paste thinly. Leave to dry for a few minutes on each side until it feels leathery.

3 Use the cutting wheel to cut a strip 2 x 13cm (¾ x 5⅛in) from the paste.

4 Pipe a thin line of piping gel along both long sides, slightly in from the edge. Start at one end of the strip and press both squares of gelatine gently into the paste. Roll the gelatine along the strip, pressing into the paste each time.

5 When the paste surrounds three sides of the gelatine, cut off the excess paste in line with the gelatine square.

6 Roll out the paste thinly. Allow to dry for a few minutes on each side. Cut out two 4cm (1½in) ovals. Cut the hole for the handle towards one side of each oval using the 1cm (⅜in) oval cutter.

7 Cut out two of the blossoms.

8 Spread a little piping gel on the back of each oval and press into place at the top of the bag to form the handle.

9 Attach a blossom to each gelatine side of the bag with a little piping gel.

Alan
The letter on the piggy's tummy can be changed to the initial of the recipient.

PIGGY

Instructions:

1 Make a basic body in peach as shown on page 20. Insert a cocktail stick and use the pointed tool to make two holes in the front for the legs.

2 Roll 20g (⅔oz) of peach coloured paste into a smooth ball for the head. Make two holes for the eyes with the pointed tool.

3 For the snout, roll 5g (⅙oz) of peach coloured paste into a smooth ball and flatten it slightly. Using a little glue, attach it to the front of the head. Insert the pointed tool and make two holes for the snout.

4 Roll 20g (⅔oz) of peach coloured paste into a ball and cut it into four pieces for the feet. Roll each piece into a ball and then press it gently into the form of a flattened disc. Mark it as shown.

5 For the legs, cut two 7cm (2¾in) lengths of chenille stick and add glue to each end. Attach a foot to one end and insert the other end into the body, then repeat with the other leg and foot.

6 Bend a 14cm (5½in) orange chenille stick in half for the arms. Add a little sugar glue to each end and attach a foot. Bend the chenille stick around the back of the cocktail stick, then glue it in place, bringing the feet down beside the body.

7 Push the head on to the cocktail stick using a little sugar glue. Press down firmly.

8 Roll 2g (¹⁄₁₂oz) of peach coloured paste into a smooth ball, then cut it in half and roll each piece into a ball again. Push the rounded end of a pointed tool into one ball. Without taking the tool out, glue the bottom part of the ear and place it on the top of the head firmly. Pinch the top of the paste to make a pointed ear then remove the tool. Repeat for the second ear.

9 Twist 10cm (4in) of pipe cleaner around the pointed tool, then glue and push one end into the base of the body at the back for a curly tail.

10 Cut out a heart from jade paste using the heart cutter and attach it to the tummy with sugar glue.

11 Using the cutters, cut out one letter and five tiny blossoms from white paste. Glue the letter on top of the heart and secure the blossoms in place with green stamens.

Materials:

100g (3½oz) peach coloured modelling paste

Small amounts of jade and white modelling paste

Two orange chenille sticks

Two white stamens

Green stamens or sugar beads

Cocktail stick

Tools:

Thin palette knife

Cutters: small heart, tiny blossom, alphabet letter

Small pair of scissors

Fine black fibre-tip pen

Sugar paste

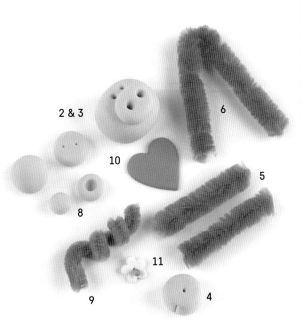

2 & 3   6   10   5   8   11   9   4

166

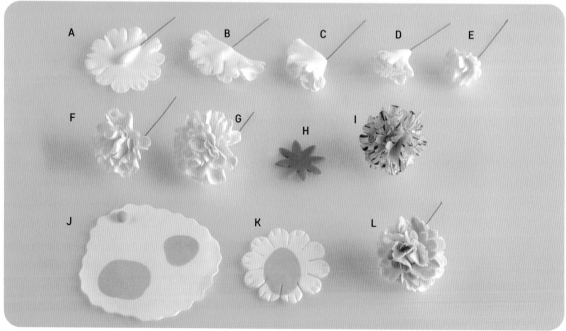

CARNATION

Materials:

Mexican (flower/gum) paste in white, green and pink

Powdered food colour: pink

Tools:

Carnation cutter: 35mm (1⅜in)

Small daisy cutter

26g wires: green (cut into quarter-lengths)

Paintbrushes: size 2/0 round, 12mm (½in) flat

Mexican foam balling pad

Instructions:

Striped flowers

1 With Mexican paste, form a bud shape on the end of a hooked 26g wire on a non-stick surface, roll out some white paste quite thinly and cut out a carnation shape using the largest cutter. Lay a mini modelling tool on the edge of the petals and roll backwards and forwards to frill and flute. Ensure you use plenty of cornflour to stop the paste and tools from sticking (A).

2 Thread the wired bud down through the centre of the prepared petal. Paint a little sugar glue on one half of the petal, fold the petal in half and squash it securely over the bud (B).

3 Now divide the petal into thirds. Paint sugar glue over the middle third and fold the third on the right side up and across the petal at a 45-degree angle (C).

4 Flip the flower over and do the same on the other side (D).

5 Squash the petals around the base of the flower to secure (E). Leave to dry.

6 Prepare two more petals in the same way as the first.

Carnation Arrangement

Once you have made a number of the flowers, put some fondant (sugarpaste) into a small container, trim the stems to length and push them into this icing to make a beautiful arrangement.

Thread the wire down through the middle of the second layer of petals and squash the petals in place behind the first petal using sugar glue to stick (F).

7 Thread the wire down through the middle of the third layer of petals and squash the petals in place behind second layer of petals, using sugar glue to stick (G).

8 Using green paste, cut out two small daisy shapes. Soften the edges with a ball tool on a Mexican foam pad, then thread them up one at a time on to the wire before sticking it behind the flower. Leave to dry (H).

9 Mix a little pink paste food colour with white alcohol, and use the round brush to paint lots of little stripes over the edges of the petals (I).

Pink variegated flowers

10 Take a ball of pink paste, place it on a flattened piece of white paste and roll with a small rolling pin to blend the colours together (J).

11 Cut out a carnation shape and prepare it as detailed in step 1 (K).

12 Prepare two more petals and prepare the flower as described above in steps 2–8. Once dry, dust the edges with a little pink powdered food colour (L).

This cute fairy is perfect for the Christmas table with her gift of a yellow sweet. If you just want her to be a winter fairy, make her in white fondant (sugarpaste), rather than red, white and green.

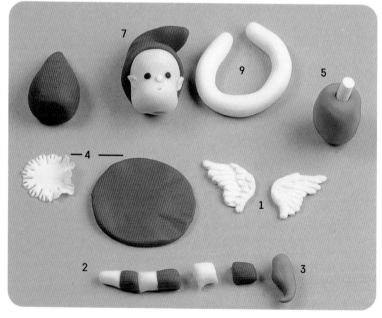

CHRISTMAS FAIRY

Materials:

10g (⅓oz) flesh-coloured fondant (sugarpaste) for the head

Green fondant (sugarpaste): 10g (⅓oz) for the body and 10g (⅓oz) for the arms and feet

Red fondant (sugarpaste): 10g (⅓oz) for the skirt and legs and 10g (⅓oz) for the hat

10g (⅓oz) white fondant (sugarpaste) for the legs, skirt, fluff and hat

10g (⅓oz) modelling paste for the wings

Candy stick

Tiny amount of black fondant (sugarpaste) for the eyes

Edible pearl white powder colour

Tools:

Multi-mould for bird wings

56mm (2¼in) circle cutter

Carnation cutter

Sieve, sugarcraft gun or garlic press

Non-stick rolling pin

Small drinking straw

Thin palette knife

Plastic sandwich bag

Dusting brush

Water brush

Dresden tool or cocktail stick

Tissue paper

Instructions:

1 For the wings, press the white modelling paste into the bird wing mould. Remove from the mould and brush with edible pearl white powder. Leave to dry for a few hours or overnight.

2 For the legs, make a red sausage, and a white sausage of fondant (sugarpaste), each the size and length wanted for legs. Cut each leg into small segments and put these in a plastic bag to keep them soft. Stick red and white segments together alternately and form two stripey legs. Roll very gently to get the segments attached smoothly (only dampen very slightly if the pieces refuse to stick). Stick the tops of the legs together, side by side.

3 For the shoes, make two pea-sized pieces of green fondant (sugarpaste) and shape each one to a point. Dampen the ends of the legs and attach the shoes.

4 For the skirt, roll out red fondant (sugarpaste) and cut out a circle using the circle cutter. Frill over the edge with a cocktail stick. Roll out white fondant (sugarpaste) and cut out a carnation. Frill around the edge as before. Dampen under the two skirt layers and stick them on top of the legs.

5 Make an egg shape of green fondant (sugarpaste) for the body with a candy stick for support, slightly sticking out. Dampen the bottom of the body and stick it on top of the skirt.

6 Divide the rest of the green fondant (sugarpaste) and form two carrot shapes for the arms. Bend to form the elbows and flatten the hands. Attach to the body.

7 Make the head following step 7, page 39. Make a cone shape from red fondant (sugarpaste) for the hat. Hollow the fat end by pressing with your finger and thumb until it fits over the back of the head. Dampen the inside and attach to the head. Bend the point of the hat over to one side.

8 Dampen the end of the candy stick neck and attach the head.

9 Roll a long sausage of white fondant (sugarpaste) and attach round the edge of the hat.

10 Attach the wings with thick edible glue/gunge. Prop them up with scrunched-up tissue paper until the glue is dry.

11 To make pompoms, push a little white fondant (sugarpaste) through a sieve, sugarcraft gun or garlic press. Dampen the end of the hat and the centre of the chest and attach the pompoms.

Spotted Our Woodpecker?
To make a Spotted Woodpecker, make the body in white and the wings in black. Lay thin strips of white across the pointed ends of the wings for stripes and press in. Mark the feathers as before.

GREEN WOODPECKER

Instructions:

1 To make the body, roll the pale green fondant (sugarpaste) to a pointed cone approximately 8cm (3in) long. Roll it between your two fingers to form the neck at the rounded end, and shape it so that the head is up and the body and tail are straight. Mark some feathers on the tail with the Dresden tool.

2 For the wings, roll two large pea-sized pieces of darker green fondant (sugarpaste) into carrot shapes, each 4cm (1½in) long. Flatten them slightly and mark the feathers on the wings with the Dresden tool. Attach them to the body.

3 To make the beak and mask, form some black modelling paste into a 3cm (1¼in) long cone. At the fat end, make a cut to form a 'Y' and shape the cut ends to form points, keeping the total length at 3cm (1¼in). Dampen inside the top of the 'Y' and stick it to the front of head, smoothing the side pieces in to look like a mask, with the point forming the beak.

4 Make two tiny balls each of white and black fondant (sugarpaste) for the eyes. Stick the black on top of the white, and then attach them to the mask.

5 Make a small pea-sized ball of red fondant (sugarpaste), then shape and flatten it to a long, slightly rounded triangle. Attach on to the top of the head for the bird's crown.

Materials:

25g (just under1oz) pale green fondant (sugarpaste)

Small amounts of darker green and red fondant (sugarpaste)

Small amount of black modelling paste

Tools:

Dresden tool

FRANKIE STEIN

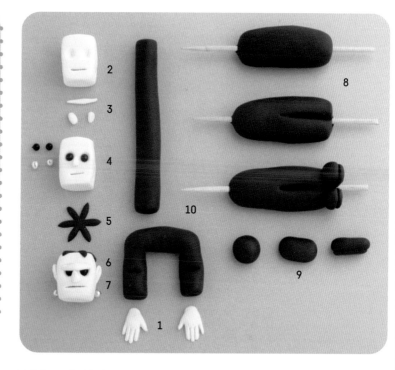

Instructions:

1 Use the Dresden tool to push a small, pea-sized piece of pale green modelling paste into the large hands on the mould. Take the hands out of the mould straight away and leave to dry for a short time.

2 For the head, shape 10g (⅜oz) of pale green modelling paste to form an oblong 2.5 x1.5cm (1 x ½in). Sharpen the edges by pinching them. Mark the eye sockets with the ball tool and mark the mouth with the knife.

3 Make a tiny sausage of pale green modelling paste, 1.5cm (½in) long, for a single eyebrow. Make two tiny, green balls for the ears.

4 Insert black sugar pearls in the eye sockets. Shape a tiny nose triangle and stick it on the face.

5 Roll out the black modelling paste thinly. Cut out a six-petal flower and stick it on top of the head for hair.

6 Stick the single eyebrow in place, shading the tops of the eyes. Dampen the sides of the head in line with the nose and stick on the ears. Press them in the middle with the Dresden tool.

7 Mark a hole on each side of the head for the neck bolts. Dampen and insert the silver sugar pearls.

8 For the body and legs, shape 20g (¾oz) of black modelling paste into a 5cm (2in) sausage. Insert the stick right through. Mark the legs with the Dresden tool or a knife.

9 Make two 2g (1⁄16oz) balls in black for the boots. Shape them into ovals.

Mark around the soles with a knife and attach them to the legs.

10 For the arms, shape 15g (½oz) of black modelling paste into a 10cm (4in) sausage. Bend to form the angles as shown, pinching the corners to make the shoulders. Make a hole in each end for the hands. Press the knife or the Dresden tool in halfway down each arm for the elbows. Bend the arms forward from the elbows.

11 Dampen the top of the body. Place the arms on the stick and push them down to join on to the body. Press a hollow in the front centre of the arms for the head. Dampen and attach the head.

12 Dampen the ends of the hands and attach them to the arms.

13 Allow to dry, lying the model down until the head is secure.

ELF BOOTS

Materials:

Mexican (flower/gum) paste in white and red

Tiny silver balls

Piping gel/edible glue

Tools:

Small non-stick rolling pin

3cm (1¼in) and 4cm (1½in) leaf/petal cutters

Multi-mould tiara

Music stave cutter

Dresden tool

Small sharp pointed scissors

Waterbrush/small paintbrush and water

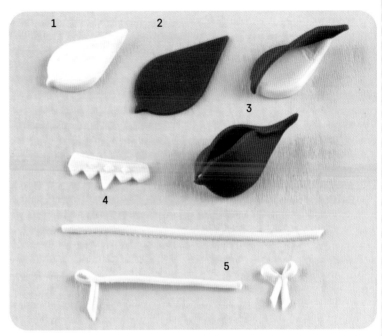

Instructions:

1 Roll out the white paste to a thickness of 1mm (¹⁄₂₀in). Cut out a 3cm (1¼in) leaf/petal shape for the sole.

2 Roll out the red paste thinly. Allow to dry slightly on each side until the paste feels leathery. Cut out two 4cm (1½in) leaf/petal shapes.

3 Dampen the sides of the sole. Attach the red leaf/petal shapes to the sole, starting at the toe end, gently pressing the paste carefully to the sides of the sole. Use the Dresden tool to help shape the boot from the inside. Dampen the heel end and along the top at the front and press together, leaving the wide end open on top.

4 Make two white tiaras from the multi-mould using white paste. Stick them around the top of the boot with the points facing down.

5 Roll out the white paste thinly. Leave it to dry for a few minutes until it feels leathery, turning it over occasionally. Cut out a short strip using the music stave cutter. Dampen a point a little way along the strip. Form a tiny loop and tail by bringing the end over to the dampened point, press in and bend the tail away from the loop. Repeat, bringing the other end in to the same point to form another loop and tail. Cut the tails to the length you want using sharp pointed scissors. Dampen the back of the boot to attach the bow.

6 Glue some tiny silver sugar balls to the point of the shoe with a little piping gel or edible glue.

Elfin Fashion

You could also make the boot in brown with tiny gold balls and mark lace holes with a no. 1 piping tube. Cut the zigzag top with sharp pointed scissors.

SKIING

Materials:

- Modelling paste: blue, red, black, white, flesh
- Rice paper
- Edible ink pen (any colour)
- Sugar glue
- Edible red dust

Tools:

- Marzipan/plastic spacers, 1.3cm (½in) depth
- Non-stick rolling pin
- Circle cutter, 2.5cm (1in)
- Square cutter, 4cm (1½in)
- Smoother
- Small paintbrush
- Small drinking straws x 2
- Craft knife
- Scriber
- Quilting tool/stitching wheel or cocktail stick
- Ball tool
- Mini ball tool
- Small scissors
- Cutting wheel
- Piping tube no. 3 or 4, 17
- Kitchen paper

Hit the Slopes

Whoops! The fun alternative (opposite, above) was made by spraying a ball of white sugar paste with edible lustre spray in pearl, with the boots and skis sticking out. It's a human snowball!

1

2

3

4

5

6

7

8

9

10

11

Instructions:

1 Make a pair of skis out of rice paper. Using an edible ink pen, draw two rectangles 9 x 1cm (3½ x ½in) on to the rice paper and cut out with the scissors. Cut one end of each ski into a point and lightly curl the ends by pulling the paper through between closed scissors and our thumb.

2 For each leg and boot use one and a half circles of blue paste and roll to a length of 7.5cm (3in). Texture the outer side of each leg, from top to bottom, with a quilting tool/stitching wheel or cocktail stick, bend at the knee and heel, and model a foot at the end of each leg.

3 Cut out two circles of blue paste for the body and roll into a pear shape, marking on a zip with the cutting wheel. Push a thumb up into the wide end of the pear to create a hollow. Secure on to the tops of the legs with sugar glue.

4 Use a pea-sized ball of blue paste for the collar, roll into a ball and flatten slightly. Mark on some vertical lines on the outer edge with the cutting wheel and secure to the top of the body with sugar glue.

5 For the head, use half a circle of flesh-coloured paste rolled into a ball with a recess in the centre. Add on a nose by rolling out some paste thinly and use no. 3 or 4 piping tubes to cut out a circle. Roll into a ball and secure into the recess in the centre of the head, using sugar glue. For the scarf, roll out some red paste, cut out a square using the 4cm (1½in) cutter and cut off a triangle (see opposite). Position it under the nose and add movement by twisting it slightly.

6 Make sunglasses by rolling out a very small amount of black paste and cutting out two circles using a no.17 piping tube. Remove the top edge of each circle with a cutting wheel and secure each one either side of the nose. Add two thin sausage shapes of paste either side of the head to make the glasses' arms.

7 For the hat, roll out some blue paste thinly. Roll four thin sausage shapes of white paste and place these across each other, like an asterisk on the blue paste. Use a rolling pin to blend the colours together, then cut out a circle using the 2.5cm (1in) cutter. Secure to the top of the head with sugar glue. Roll a tiny amount of blue paste into a ball to make the bobble and secure to the hat with sugar glue.

8 For the hair, roll three very small balls of flesh-coloured paste into teardrop shapes and secure to the top of the head with sugar glue.

9 For the arms, use one circle of blue paste and roll into a tapered sausage shape 10cm (4in) long. Cut it in half to make two arms, indent at one end with the ball tool (this is where the hands will go) and add stitch detail as for the legs in step 2. Secure to the body with sugar glue.

10 For the gloves, take a little black paste and model mitten shapes. Use a craft knife to cut out a small triangle from the round shape to make a thumb. Round off the sharp edges with a scriber. Attach them to the arms with sugar glue and wrap them around each small drinking straw (ski pole).

11 Add a small black ball of paste to the top of each ski pole. Use the no.17 piping tube as a size guide and secure with sugar glue. Give your skier rosy cheeks using a little edible red dust and a small paintbrush.

BASSETT HOUND

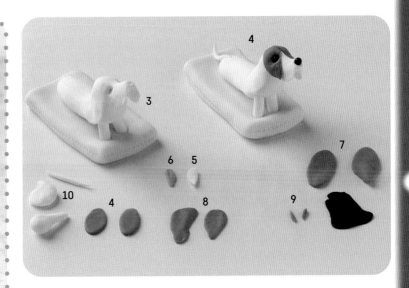

Materials:

- 30g (1oz) yellow modelling paste
- 25g (just under 1oz) white modelling paste
- Small amounts of tan, black and pink modelling paste
- Edible candy sticks
- Edible black sugar pearls

Tools:

- 2cm (¾in) oval cutter
- Dresden tool
- Water brush
- Thin palette knife
- Stitching wheel
- Small non-stick rolling pin

Instructions:

1 Shape the yellow modelling paste into a pillow 8 x 3cm (3⅛ x 1¼in). Mark around the edge with the stitching wheel. At one end, push in two 2cm (¾in) edible candy sticks vertically, close together for the dog's front legs.

2 Shape 15g (½oz) of white paste to a 6cm (2⅜in) sausage for the body. Bend in the middle, and then bend one end again to make a 'Z' shape. The smaller end will become the head.

3 Pinch down the sides of the head to form the muzzle, and gently shape the head to form a forehead. Dampen the top of the front legs and press the chest on to the tops of the legs.

4 Roll out tan paste thinly and cut out two 2cm (¾in) ovals. Dampen and stick on either side of the face as shown. Mark the eyes and nose with a Dresden tool and insert edible black sugar pearls.

5 Make a tiny short pointed cone of white paste for the tail and stick it on.

6 Make a tiny pink flattened cone for the tongue. Attach it so that it sticks out as shown. Make another small cone of white paste for the bottom jaw, and stick that in place under the tongue.

7 Roll out the black and tan paste thinly. Cut two 3cm (1¼in) ovals of tan for the ears and small irregular shapes of both colours to stick on to the body.

8 Stick the ears to the sides of the head, hanging straight down.

9 Make two tiny sausages of paste for the eyebrows. Stick above the eyes.

10 Shape two 3g (¹⁄₁₀oz) pieces of white paste to 3cm (1¼in) carrot shapes for back legs; flatten the fat end of each and curve it towards the paw. Dampen and stick to the sides of the back end of the body, toes facing forwards.

ANGEL

Materials:

- 100g (3½oz) white modelling paste
- 25g (⅚oz) flesh-coloured modelling paste
- Small amount of yellow royal icing
- Two silver chenille sticks
- White glitter
- Pale pink dusting powder
- Butterfly wings
- Craft jewels
- Cocktail stick
- 5cm (2in) length of strong wire

Tools:

- Fine black fibre-tip pen
- Cutters: Garrett frill, 2.5cm (1in) blossom, medium star
- No. 2 icing nozzle and piping bag
- Sugar glue

4/10

5

6

9

12

8

13

7

14

Instructions:

1 Make a basic body in white as shown on page 20 and insert an 8cm (3¼in) cocktail stick. Make two holes in the front for the legs using the pointed tool.

2 Roll 20g (⅔oz) of flesh-coloured paste into a smooth ball for the head. Use a pointed tool to make a hole for the nose and use the smiley tool to mark the mouth.

3 Roll a small ball of flesh-coloured paste into a cone for the nose. Using a little glue, secure the pointed end into the head. When the head is completely dry, draw on the eyes using a fine black fibre-tip pen and dust the cheeks with the pink dusting powder.

4 Roll out a small amount of white paste and cut out two leg frills using the blossom cutter. Frill the edge of both pieces with the rounded end of the pointed tool, then use a little glue to secure them over the leg holes. Use the pointed tool to remake the holes.

5 Cut two 7.5cm (3in) lengths of chenille stick to make the legs. Cut a 12g (⁵⁄₁₂oz) ball of white paste in half to make two oval shoes. Lightly glue one end of a length of chenille stick and insert it into one shoe. Repeat with the other leg and shoe. Lightly glue the shoes and cover with the white glitter. Shake off the excess, then glue the ends of the legs and insert them into the body.

6 Cut out two small blossoms, add a craft jewel and glue one on the top of each shoe.

7 To make the skirts, cut out three circles of white paste using the Garrett frill cutter. Frill the edges of the circles with the rounded end of the pointed tool.

8 Using the large end of the No. 2 icing nozzle, cut out a hole in the middle of two of the frills. Add glue to the body just above the leg frills. Pull each of the two skirts down over the cocktail stick and secure in place. Lightly glue the top of the body, pull the third frill down over the top of the cocktail stick and gently ease the paste down as shown, covering the top of the body.

9 Cut a 3g (⅛oz) ball of flesh-coloured paste in half to make two oval hands. Add a little sugar glue to each end of a 12cm (4¾in) length of chenille stick and attach the hands. Bend the chenille stick around the back of the cocktail stick and glue in place, bringing the arms down. Position arms when dry.

10 Roll out some white paste and cut two medium size blossoms for the neck frills. Frill the edges as before, then place the frills on individually. Press down at the front and back to secure them over the chenille stick. Glue the head on firmly.

11 With a small amount of pale yellow royal icing, pipe small circles all over the head for hair.

12 To make the halo, cut a 12cm (4¾in) piece of silver chenille stick and bend the top around in a circle. Push the other end into the top of the head.

13 For the wand, cut out two medium stars from white paste. Using a little sugar glue, place the 5cm (2in) length of wire in the middle of one star and place the other star on top. Press down to secure. Cover the star with a little glue and sprinkle with glitter. Leave to dry before pushing the completed wand gently into a hand.

14 Secure the wings on the back of the body with a small amount of royal icing, then decorate your angel with craft jewels.

The lioness is made in the same way as the lion, but the head is made from a yellow ball as she does not have a mane.

LION

Materials:

50g (1¾oz) golden yellow
    fondant (sugarpaste)

15g (½oz) orange fondant
    (sugarpaste)

Small amounts of black and
    brown fondant (sugarpaste)

Candy stick

Tools:

Cocktail stick

Sharp pointed scissors

Thin palette knife

Heart cutter, 2.5cm (1in)

Instructions:

1 Divide the yellow paste, taking about 25g (just under 1oz) for the body. Form this into an egg shape and add a candy stick for support. Divide the rest of the paste into about 5g (1/6oz) each for the front legs, tail and face, and the rest for the back legs.

2 Form the piece for the back legs into two cones. Flatten them slightly, mark toes with a cocktail stick and join them on to the body.

3 For the front legs, attach two sausage shapes, the same height as the body. Mark lines on the end of each foot to form paws.

4 To make the mane, form a ball of orange paste and squash it slightly to make a fat circle. Mark soft indents around the edge with a cocktail stick. Attach it to the top of the body.

5 For the face, cut out a heart shape from yellow paste, using the heart

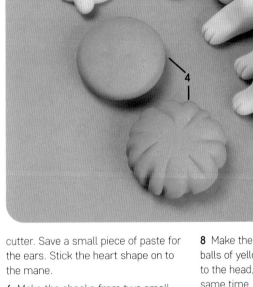

cutter. Save a small piece of paste for the ears. Stick the heart shape on to the mane.

6 Make the cheeks from two small yellow ovals. Mark them with a cocktail stick for the whiskers and attach them to the heart-shaped face.

7 Form the nose from a small triangle of brown paste and the eyes from two tiny balls of black paste. Attach these to the face.

8 Make the ears from two small balls of yellow paste. Stick them on to the head, cupping them at the same time.

9 Make a long, thin sausage for the tail. Flatten one end slightly, then cut with a knife or scissors to make the end look fluffy. Attach the tail.

COUNTRY BRIDE

Materials:

Modelling paste: flesh-coloured: 13g (½oz); green:
pinhead-sized piece; brown and orange: 5g (⅙oz);
white: 63g (2¹⁰⁄₁₀oz); yellow: tiny piece; pale pink:
3g (¹⁄₁₀oz); green: pea-sized piece

Sugar/spaghetti sticks

Edible glue/pasteurised egg white

White and brown gel
food colouring

Pink dusting powder

Small dragées or nonpareils

Tools:

Cutting mat

Non-stick rolling pin

Scalpel/craft knife

Styrofoam

Piping nozzle (tube)

Small paintbrush

Toothpick

Dresden tool/skewer

Small paintbrush

Instructions:

1 Using 10g (⅓oz) of flesh-coloured
paste, make a cone-shaped head with
green eyes, following steps 1–5, page
31. Paint the eyelashes and eyebrows
with brown gel food colouring.

2 Using 60g (2oz) of white paste,
make the dress following step 7, page
31. Indent the top of the dress with
your index finger to create a neckline.
Bend the dress into a sitting position
over the edge of a piece of styrofoam.
Mark a line around the waist and
pull a Dresden tool/skewer upwards
from the waist to form pleats on the
bodice. Mark random pleats on the
skirt of the dress and attach dragées
or nonpareils with edible glue. Push a
sugar stick/spaghetti through the top
to protrude 1.5cm (⅔in).

3 Make shoes from 3g (¹⁄₁₀oz) of
white paste, following step 8,
page 31.

4 For the neck, roll a small piece
of flesh-coloured paste into a cone.
Place it over the sugar stick/spaghetti
and flatten it onto the top of the
dress. Attach with glue.

5 Form arms and hands, following
step 10, page 31. Attach them to the
sides of the body, bending the arms

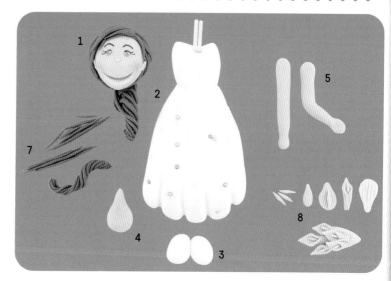

forward and placing the bride's hands
in her lap.

6 Attach the head to the neck with
edible glue.

7 For the hair, make tapered
sausages from 5g (⅙oz) of brown
and orange paste and glue them to
the head, starting from the forehead,
placing them with a side parting
towards the neck. Roll a few tapered
sausages and pinch them at one end
to stick them together. Twist the
ponytail and glue it to the back of
the head, close to the neck, and let it

hang over the bride's shoulder. Roll a
few short tapered sausages to make
a fringe.

8 Make five pink arum lilies by rolling
tiny sausages from yellow paste.
Divide 3g (¹⁄₁₀oz) of white paste into
smaller pieces and roll into cones.
Flatten and roll each cone around
a yellow sausage, attaching the
overlapping side with edible glue/egg
white. Make a cone from green paste;
mark straight lines with a knife like a
bunch of stems. Glue the lilies to the
stems. Place them on the bride's lap.

DENIM BAG

Materials:

- Mexican (flower/gum) paste in beige and blue
- Yellow and white food colouring (powder or paste) and food grade alcohol or water
- Tiny gold-coloured sugar balls
- Piping gel

Tools:

- Small, non-stick rolling pin
- 6cm (2⅜in) and 1cm (⅜in) square cutters
- 2cm (¾in) and 1.5cm (⅝in) circle cutters
- Cutting wheel
- Fine stitching wheel
- Fine paintbrush

Instructions:

1 To make the handles, roll out the beige paste thinly. Cut out two 2cm (¾in) circles and cut the centres out with the 1.5cm (⅝in) circle cutter. Allow to dry until the handles hold their shape.

2 Roll out the blue paste thinly. Cut out one 6cm (2⅜in) square and two 1cm (⅜in) squares.

3 Fold the large square in half and run the fine stitching wheel down the sides to join them.

4 Cut two corners from each of the smaller squares. Mark around the edges with the stitching wheel to make pockets. Stick the pockets on to one side of the bag.

5 Mix white food colouring with a few drops of alcohol or water. Add a small amount of yellow food colouring. The white colouring will make the yellow show up on the blue paste. Paint along the lines of stitching down the sides and on the pockets.

6 Carefully gather the top of the bag together with little folds. Press gently then cut through the top with the 2cm (¾in) circle cutter.

7 Dampen the curved cut edge and attach the handles.

8 Attach tiny gold sugar balls on the corners of the bag and pockets using small dots of piping gel.

ELEPHANT

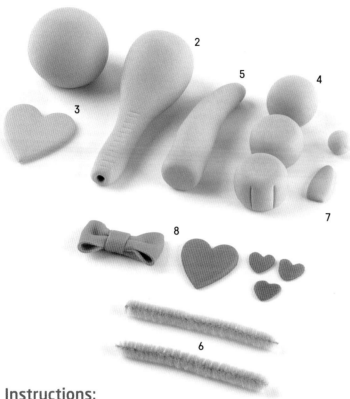

Materials:

110g (3⅞oz) grey
   modelling paste
Dark pink modelling paste
One grey chenille stick
Two white stamens
Miniature roses
Cocktail stick

Tools:

Pointed tool
Smiley tool/drinking straw
Paintbrushes
Texture frilling tool
Ball tool
Small, non-stick rolling pin
Thin palette knife
Small pair of scissors
Cutters: large heart, tiny heart
Fine black fibre-tip pen
Sugar glue

Instructions:

1 Make a basic body in grey, as shown on page 20, then make two holes in the front for the legs with the pointed tool.

2 Make the head by rolling 20g (⅔oz) of grey paste into a ball, and shaping as shown. Use a pointed tool to make a hole in the end of the trunk and two holes for the eyes. Support the head on a cocktail stick. Turn the trunk up over the head, supporting it if necessary, and use the smiley tool to make a small mouth under the trunk. Insert stamens for the eyes, using a black pen to mark the dots. Leave to dry.

3 Roll out a small amount of grey paste and cut out two large hearts for the ears. Leave to dry.

4 Roll 20g (⅔oz) of grey paste into a ball and cut it into four pieces with the scissors. Roll each piece into a ball and press it into a flat disc. Use the palette knife to mark each as shown to make the feet. Place one on each side of the body.

5 Make the arms by rolling 20g (⅔oz) of grey paste into a smooth ball and cutting it in half with scissors, then rolling each half into a sausage shape the length of the body from the shoulder to the top of the foot. Glue each in place.

6 To make the legs, cut two 7cm (2¾in) lengths of chenille stick. Add sugar glue to each end, attach a foot to one end and insert the other end into the body. Repeat with the other leg and foot.

7 Attach the head to the body with a little glue, then attach the ears. Flatten a small ball of grey fondant (sugarpaste) and attach it to the body as a tail.

8 Roll out a small amount of dark pink fondant (sugarpaste) and cut out tiny pink hearts. Glue them to the feet and tummy. Make a bow from the fondant (sugarpaste) and attach it below the head with sugar glue.

Elegant Roses

Additional curl can be added to the top edges of the rose petals by rolling them backwards with a mini modelling tool. Secure to a sugar plaque with royal icing for a beautiful cake topper.

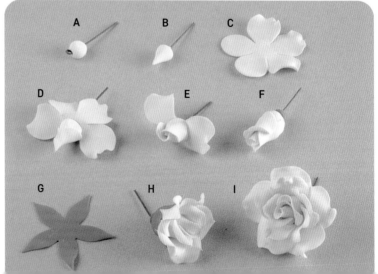

ROSE

Materials:

Mexican (flower/gum) paste in white,
  ivory and green

Powdered food colour: yellow, green

Paintbrushes: size 2/0 round, 12mm (½in)

Tools:

Extremely large five-petal blossom cutter:
  75mm (3in)

Extremely large calyx cutter: 60mm (2⅜in)

20g wires: green (cut into quarter-lengths)

Paintbrushes: size 2/0 round, 12mm (½in) flat

Stem tape: green

Mexican foam balling pad

Ball or bone tool

Dresden tool

Rose leaf plunger cutter: 25mm (1in)

Instructions:

1 With long-nosed pliers, bend a hook on the end of a 20g wire. Roll a small marble-sized ball of white paste, moisten the hook with sugar glue, then pull the wire down through the centre of the ball of paste (A).

2 With your fingers, roll the top of the ball of paste to form a pointed cone shape. Leave to dry (B).

3 On a non-stick surface, roll out some ivory paste quite thinly. Cut out a five-petal blossom shape using the extremely large cutter. Place the shape on a Mexican foam balling pad then soften and shape the edges of the petals by rubbing a ball or bone tool around the outer edge of each petal (C).

4 Use a round paintbrush to paint the centre of the blossom shape with sugar glue. Pull the wired cone down through the centre of the flower and stick one petal tightly around the cone (D).

5 Select a pair of petals opposite one another, and apply sugar glue three-quarters of the way up the sides of the petals. Stick each petal in turn to the side of the cone, starting with the right-hand side of each petal, then sticking the left-hand side of each petal down so that it overlaps the edge of the opposite petal (E).

6 Select the remaining two petals and stick around the bud in the same way as before, spiralling the petals around. This forms the bud stage of a rose. Roll a tiny ball of green paste, thread on to the wire and stick it at the base of the rose (F).

7 To make a medium-sized rose, cut out and prepare another set of petals, this time cupping each petal with a ball tool. Thread them on to the wire and move them behind the bud. Glue each petal on in turn so that they spiral around, with the right-hand side of each petal stuck down first, and the left-hand side of each subsequent petal overlapping the previous one (H). Add a green ball of paste as before.

8 Cut out a calyx shape from green paste (G), place it on a foam pad and soften the edges with a ball tool. Moisten it with sugar glue and stick it to the base of the rose, using a Dresden tool to tuck the paste in around the little green ball of paste that was previously added to the base of the flower (H).

9 A larger rose can be achieved by adding a further set of petals in the same way before adding on the calyx (I).

10 Once dry, use a flat brush to dust the edges and down in between some of the petals with a little yellow powdered food colour (see detail opposite) and add in a little green colouring. Assemble by taping the stems together with stem tape. Make some rose leaves with a rose leaf plunger cutter and add these to the arrangement.

This beautiful fairy godmother looks as though she could fix anything for you! She would make a lovely gift for a godmother or just a friend who has helped you out.

FAIRY GODMOTHER

Materials:

Pink modelling paste:
35g (1¼oz) for the body, 10g
(⅓oz) for the arms and cape

5g (⅙oz) flesh-coloured
fondant (sugarpaste)

5g (⅙oz) white
fondant (sugarpaste)

Candy stick

Edible powder food colour pearl
white

Egg white

Tools:

Garrett frill cutter (large fluted
round cutter)

Large butterfly cutter

Tiny star cutter

Scissors

Dusting brush

Non-stick rolling pin

Small drinking straw

Thin palette knife

Plastic sandwich bag

Water brush

Dresden tool or cocktail stick

Instructions:

1 For the wings, roll out the white fondant and cut out a large butterfly and a tiny star. Gently brush pearl white powder food colour over the surfaces. Frill over the edge of the butterfly using a Dresden tool or cocktail stick. Leave to dry for a few hours or overnight.

2 For the body, make a pear shape from pink modelling paste with a candy stick for support, slightly sticking out for the neck.

3 For the cape, roll out pink modelling paste thinly. Cut out one garrett frill. Dampen the back of the body. Wrap the cape around the body, slightly higher at the shoulders.

4 Divide 5g (⅙oz) of the pink modelling paste and form two carrot shapes for the arms. Bend to form the elbows, and flatten the hands. Attach to the body.

5 Attach the wings with thick edible glue. Prop them up with scrunched-up paper tissue until the glue is dry. Place the star on one hand.

6 To make the head follow step 7, page 39.

7 For the hair, make small carrots of white fondant (sugarpaste). Attach to the head, shaping into a style. Mark extra strands of hair with a Dresden tool or cocktail stick. Attach a pea-sized piece to form a bun on top.

8 Use thick edible glue to stick the head on top of the neck.

Spread Your Wings
Try your hand at modelling this popular pet in fondant (sugarpaste) – no birdcage required!

COCKATOO

Wing template

Materials:

25g (just under 1oz) white fondant (sugarpaste)

Small amounts of yellow, grey and black fondant (sugarpaste)

Edible wafer paper

Chocolate stick or candy stick

Tools:

Wing template

Dresden tool/cocktail stick

Sharp knife/scissors

No. 2 piping tube

Instructions:

1 Trace the wings on to the edible wafer paper using the template. Use the Dresden tool to keep the wafer paper white. Cut out the wings with scissors.

2 For the body, make an 8cm (3in) cone out of white fondant (sugarpaste). Roll the fat end between your two fingers to make the neck and the head. Mark on the tail feathers with the Dresden tool or a cocktail stick.

3 Make the beak out of a short cone of grey fondant (sugarpaste), attach it to the head and curve downwards. Mark on the two nostrils.

4 Make the eye sockets by pushing the piping tube into the fondant (sugarpaste) head. Make two tiny balls of black fondant (sugarpaste) and stick them into the eye sockets.

5 Shape a short cone of yellow fondant (sugarpaste) for the crest. Cut into the pointed end, making at least three cuts. Attach it to the top of the head and curve the points upwards.

6 Make the feet from two small grey cones of fondant (sugarpaste). Cut the pointed end twice to form three toes or claws. Attach the feet to the candy stick, close together. Dampen the top of the feet and sit the body on top.

7 Dampen the sides of the body and attach the wings.

EVIL CLOWN

Materials:

20g (¾oz) white fondant (sugarpaste)

Small amounts of red, black, yellow, green and orange fondant (sugarpaste) (or any other mix of colours)

Edible red sugar pearls

Tools:

Dresden tool

Rolling pin

2cm (¾in) oval cutter

Fine-mesh nylon sieve or tea strainer

Small, fine palette knife

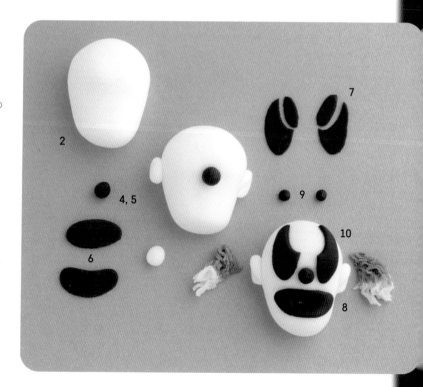

Instructions:

1 Make two tiny ovals of white fondant (sugarpaste) for the ears.

2 Roll the rest of the white paste into a ball for the head, then roll your finger across one end to make a pear shape.

3 Make a hole in the centre for the nose.

4 Attach the ears in line with the nose by pressing each oval into the head with the Dresden tool.

5 Make a small red ball of fondant (sugarpaste) for the nose. Attach it to the face.

6 Roll out some red paste thinly. for the lips. Cut a 2cm (¾in) oval and curve the ends up slightly.

7 Roll out the black fondant (sugarpaste) thinly. Cut out two 2cm (¾in) ovals. Cut each one with the edge of the oval cutter again to look like horns.

8 Attach the lips under the nose. Use the Dresden tool to mark the mouth from side to side. Attach the black horn shapes to the face.

9 Make holes for the eyes and insert red sugar pearls or red paste shaped into two pea-sized balls.

10 Choose the three colours for the hair. Press the fondant (sugarpaste) through the tea strainer in any order you choose; I put yellow through first, followed by green and then orange. Use the palette knife to cut the hair.

off the back of the tea strainer when it is the chosen length. Carefully divide it in two and stick above the ears.

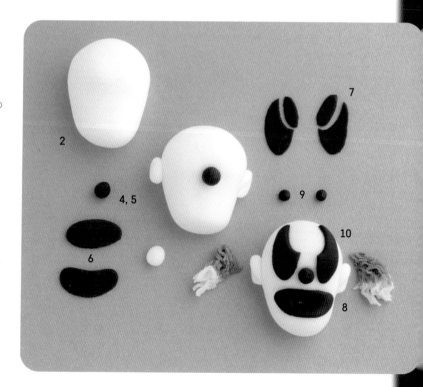

Star Spangled Stunner
Tiny edible stars could be stuck on to the blue toe piece using piping gel, to celebrate all things American.

PATRIOTIC PLATFORMS

Instructions:

1 Roll out the white paste to 2mm (¹/₁₀in) thick. Cut out a 2.5cm (1in) circle. Cut across the middle with the palette knife. Cut again at a slight angle as shown; the curve on top helps to shape the sole. Allow the heel to dry for about 30 minutes, turning it over occasionally.

2 Roll the white paste to a thickness of 1mm (¹/₂₀in). Cut out the 4cm (1½in) sole. Rest the heel end over a dowel for a few minutes to create the high-heeled shape, until the sole feels leathery.

3 To make the platform sole, roll out the different coloured pastes to 2mm (¹/₁₀in) thick. Use the shoe sole cutter to cut out just the wide, front part of the shoe in each colour. Stick them on top of each other. Cut the already cut end, angling downwards to join the ends together. Turn the platform over and stick it to the underside of the sole. Lay it on its side and attach the heel. Stand the shoe up, making sure it stands straight. If necessary, the end of the heel should still be soft enough to cut. Leave to dry for about 30 minutes.

4 Brush piping gel or edible glue over the heel. Sprinkle with edible glitter. Use a small, dry paintbrush or cotton bud to remove excess glitter.

5 Roll out the blue paste thinly. Allow to dry on each side until it feels leathery. Cut out a 2.5cm (1in) circle. Use the same cutter to cut a tiny curve off for the toe end and a larger piece off the other side of the circle.

6 Roll out the white and red paste thinly. Allow to dry on each side until the paste feels leathery. Cut strips of each colour using the music stave cutter. Use the cutter to cut the red strip again to make it thinner than the white one. Stick the white strip across the top of the blue shape to form a wide 'X', then dampen and lay the thinner red strip over the top. Use the Dresden tool to shape it. Dampen the underside edges of the blue shape, stick to the sides of the sole and allow to dry.

7 For the back piece, roll out the red paste thinly. Allow to dry slightly on each side until it feels leathery. Cut out a 2cm (¾in) square. Cut it in half diagonally. Use the Dresden tool to help shape it, then dampen the long edge and stick it around the back of the heel end of the sole. Cut the 8cm (3⅛in) ankle strap from the rest of the red paste, using the music stave cutter. Loop the strap to make a circle as shown and dampen it to attach it to the top of the triangle.

Materials:
Mexican (flower/gum) paste in white, red and blue
White edible glitter
Piping gel/edible glue

Tools:
Small non-stick rolling pin
4cm (1½in) shoe sole cutter
2.5cm (1in) circle cutter
Dowel
2cm (¾in) square cutter
Small fine palette knife
Music stave cutter
Dresden tool
Small sharp pointed scissors
Waterbrush/small paintbrush and water

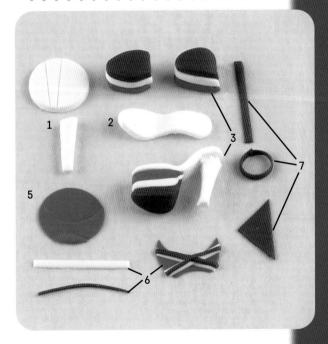

DALMATIAN

Materials:

- 30g (1oz) brown modelling paste
- 25g (just under 1oz) white modelling paste
- Small amount of red modelling paste
- Edible candy sticks
- Edible black sugar pearls
- Black food colour pen

Tools:

- Dresden tool
- Water brush
- Thin palette knife
- Cutting wheel
- Small non-stick rolling pin
- Small petal shape cutter

Instructions:

1 Shape 20g (²⁄₃oz) of brown modelling paste to a 6 x 4cm (2⅜ x 1½in) oval for the bed. Make a long sausage with 10g (⅓oz) of brown paste. Measure the length by wrapping around the bed edge (it is around 16cm (6¼in). Flatten slightly with a rolling pin. If necessary, cut along the length to neaten the edge. Cut both ends neatly, dampen and wrap around the bed, leaving a small opening to look like a dog bed.

2 Shape 15g (½oz) of white paste to a 6cm (2⅜in) sausage for the body. At one end, pinch and shape a small tail. At the other end, press and pinch to widen it slightly. Dampen the widened part and wrap it around the top of two 6cm (2⅜in) edible candy sticks. Lift the whole body and legs on to the bed. Push the legs vertically into the bed, position the body and tail to a sitting position and dampen to attach the dog to the bed.

3 For each back leg, make a 4cm (1½in) carrot using 2.5g (¹⁄₁₀oz) of white paste. Press the fat end to widen it. Bend it in the middle. Mark the toes with a knife. Dampen and attach to the base of the body.

4 Roll out red modelling paste thinly to make the bandana. Cut a 4cm (1½in) square, then cut diagonally to make a triangle. Dampen and wrap around the top of the body. Pinch together at the back of the neck.

5 Make a 5g (⅙oz) long pear shape of white paste for the head. Gently pinch down the sides of the narrow end to form the muzzle. Mark indentations for the eyes and nose using the Dresden tool and insert edible black sugar pearls. Make a tiny cone for the bottom jaw and stick it in with the rounded end under the nose. Dampen the top of the neck and push the head gently into place. Allow to dry for a couple of hours.

6 Roll out white paste thinly. Cut out two small petal shapes for ears. Attach to the back of the head, points upwards, then fold the tips forward.

7 Use the black edible food colour pen to draw random-shaped dots all over the dog. This job is much easier if the surface of the paste is fully dry.

Father Christmas
Father Christmas would be a wonderful gift in his own right.

FATHER CHRISTMAS

Materials:

80g (2¾oz) red modelling paste

25g (⅚oz) flesh-coloured modelling paste

20g (⅔oz) black modelling paste

Small amount of Mexican (flower/gum) paste in white

Gold paint

Pale pink dusting powder

One red chenille stick

White royal icing

No. 2 icing nozzle and piping bag

Tools:

Cutters: small square, 4cm (1½in) oval, 3cm (1³⁄₁₆in) circle

Fine black fibre-tip pen

Craft knife

Sugar glue

Paintbrush

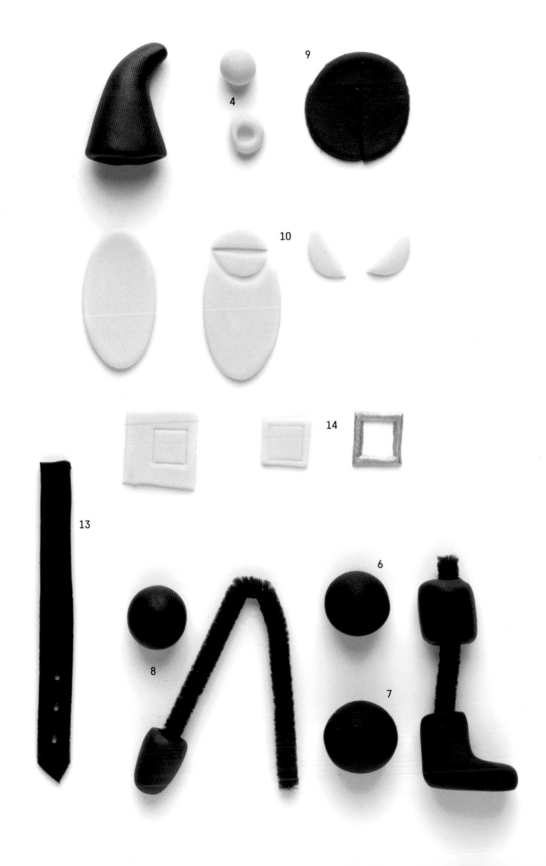

208

Instructions:

1 Make a basic body in red as shown on page 20 and insert an 8cm (3¼in) cocktail stick. Make two holes in the front for the legs using the pointed tool.

2 Roll 20g (⅔oz) of flesh-coloured paste into a smooth ball for the head. Use a pointed tool to make a hole for the nose and use the smiley tool to mark the mouth.

3 Roll a small ball of flesh-coloured paste into a cone for the nose. Using a little glue, insert the narrow end into the hole in the head.

4 For the ears, cut a 1g (¹⁄₁₆oz) ball of flesh-coloured paste in half and roll each piece into a smaller ball. Push the rounded end of a pointed tool into one ball. Glue the bottom part of the ear and place it firmly at the side of the head. Remove the tool and repeat with the other ear. Leave to dry. When the head is completely dry, mark the eyes with a fine black fibre-tip pen and dust the cheeks with pale pink dusting powder.

5 Cut two 7.5cm (3in) lengths of chenille stick for the legs.

6 To make the trousers, cut a 12g (⁵⁄₁₂oz) ball of red paste in half and roll each piece into a smaller ball. Insert a length of chenille stick through the middle of one ball and roll it into a cylinder. Repeat with the other leg. Lightly glue one end of each chenille stick and push into the body, then glue the small ball of red paste and press further on to the body. Repeat with the other leg.

7 For the boots, cut a 15g (½oz) ball of black paste in half. Roll each half into a sausage shape and turn up one end to make the boot. Glue the remaining end of the chenille stick and attach the boot. Repeat with the other boot.

8 Roll 6g (⅕oz) of red paste into a ball and cut it in half to make two oval mittens. Add sugar glue to each end of a 12cm (4¾in) length of red chenille stick and attach a mitten to each end. Bend the chenille stick around the back of the cocktail stick and glue in place. Shape the arms and hands into position when dry.

9 To make the collar, cut out a circle of red paste using the 3cm (1³⁄₁₆in) cutter. Make a small cut in the paste as shown. Using a little glue, place the collar over the cocktail stick. Push the head on firmly.

10 To make the beard, cut out an oval from white paste, trim off the end using the end of the oval cutter, and cut the removed part in half to make the moustache as shown. Secure the beard and moustache in place with a little royal icing.

11 To represent the fur and hair, pipe small circles of white royal icing on the Father Christmas as shown.

12 Roll out 10g (⅓oz) of red paste into a ball. Make it into a cone by opening out the middle with a large pointed tool and stretching the top to a point as shown, then glue the hat to the top of the head.

13 Roll a 1 x 10cm (⅜ x 4in) strip of black paste for a belt. Cut holes along one end with the narrow end of an icing nozzle and cut that end into a point. Glue in place.

14 For the buckle, roll out a small amount of white flower paste and cut a small square. Leave the square in the paste. Using a craft knife, cut a second square around the outer edge of the first one. Lift both squares using a palette knife and remove the inner one. Make a very small oval of white paste for the hook inside the buckle. Paint both gold. When dry attach to the belt with sugar glue.

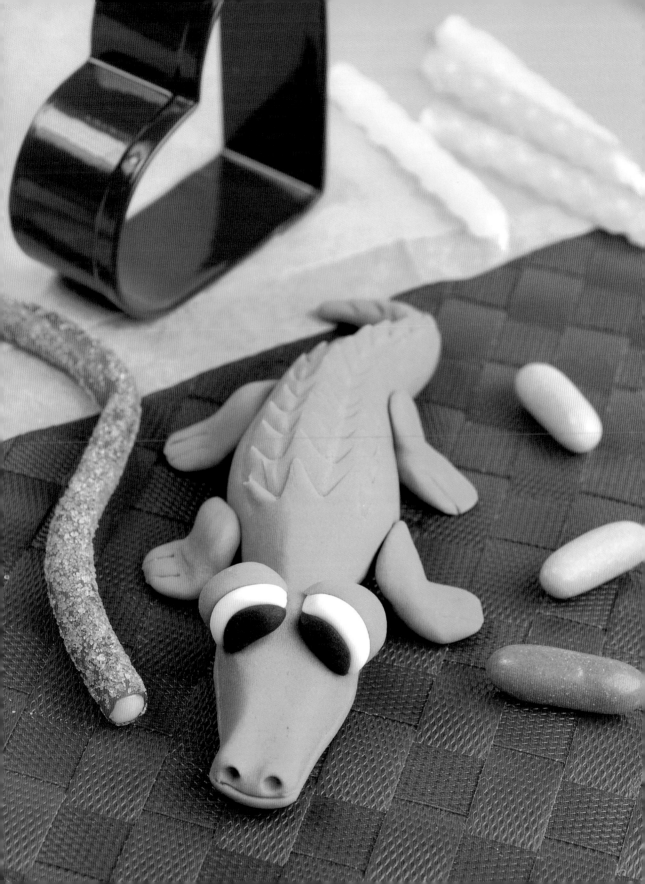

CROCODILE

Materials:

50g (1¾oz) green
   fondant (sugarpaste)
Small amounts of white and black
   fondant (sugarpaste)

Tools:

Cocktail stick
Drinking straw
Sharp pointed scissors
Thin palette knife

Instructions:

1 Make four pea-sized pieces for the feet. Roll each to make a small cone. Flatten slightly. Mark the toes with a knife.

2 To make the eyes, take one small pea-sized piece of green, press on a slightly smaller ball of white, then press on an even smaller ball of black. Cut the whole ball in half across the top.

3 Use the rest of the green paste to form a long pointed carrot shape for the body. The pointed end will form the tail. Roll the fatter end of the body between your fingers to form the head, and flatten it slightly.

4 Mark the mouth with a knife, and make two nostrils by pressing in the point of a cocktail stick.

5 Use scissors to mark small V-shapes down the crocodile's back.

6 Join the legs to the sides of the body.

7 Stick the cut edges of the eyes on top of the head.

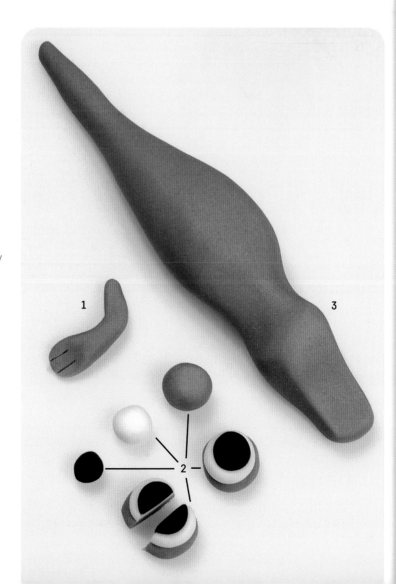

INDIAN GROOM

Materials:

Modelling paste
   Light brown flesh-coloured: 12g (½oz)
   black: small piece mustard yellow: 49g (1¾oz);
   bright pink: 10g (⅓oz)
Sugar/spaghetti sticks
Edible glue/pasteurised egg white
White and black gel food colouring
Gold dusting powder
Clear alcohol

Tools:

Cutting mat
Non-stick rolling pin
Scalpel/craft knife
Small paintbrush
Piping nozzle (tube)
Toothpick
Dresden tool/skewer

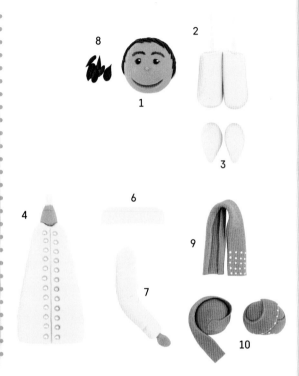

Instructions:

1 Using 10g (⅓oz) of light brown paste, make a round head with black eyes, following steps 1–5, page 31.

2 Use 10g (⅓oz) of mustard yellow paste to make trousers following step 2, page 59, but keep in mind that the trousers will only be 3cm (1¼in) long.

3 Make shoes from 3g (¹⁄₁₀oz) of yellow paste, following step 3, page 59. Pinch the fronts into sharp points. Stick two sugar/spaghetti sticks through the trouser legs into the feet, protruding 2.5cm (1in) above the trousers.

4 Roll 30g (1oz) of mustard yellow paste into a large, thick cone 7.5cm (3in) long. Flatten the cone and cut it off at the widest end. Complete by following the instructions for the jacket in step 4, page 59. It should be 6cm (2½in) long and will need longer sugar/spaghetti sticks for support.

5 Make a neck as described in step 5, page 59.

6 Make a collar from mustard yellow paste, as described in step 6, page 59, but cut the two top corners of the rectangle round instead of diagonally.

7 Make sleeves from 6g (⅕oz) of yellow and hands from a pea-sized piece of light brown paste, following steps 8 and 9, page 59.

8 Attach the head to the neck and make short hair from black modelling paste for the front of the head only.

9 Roll out 5g (⅙oz) of bright pink modelling paste thinly to make a stole. cut out a rectangle 10cm (4in) long. fold the sides inwards to resemble a fabric edge. Drape the stole over the groom's shoulder.

10 Use 5g (⅙oz) of bright pink modelling paste and make a turban by rolling half into a ball and half into a long strip, attaching as shown above.

11 Mix gold dusting powder with clear alcohol and use a toothpick to dab dots on the bottom edge of the stole, on the edge of the turban and on the buttons.

DESIGNER SATCHEL

Materials:

Mexican (flower/gum) paste coloured
   with dark brown and autumn leaf
   food colouring

Edible gold paint

Tools:

Small, non-stick
   rolling pin

5cm (2in) oval cutter

Music stave cutter

Cutting wheel

Ruler

Fine paintbrush

Cocktail stick

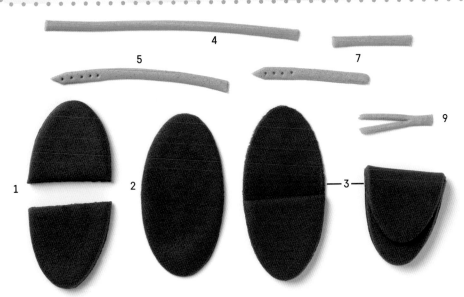

Instructions:

1 Roll the dark brown paste to 3mm (⅛in) thick. Cut out the 5cm (2in) oval. Cut in half.

2 Roll the dark brown paste thinly. Cut another 5cm (2in) oval.

3 Dampen the thin oval. Stick the thick half-oval on top then fold the rest of the thin oval over the front to create the bag.

4 Roll the autumn leaf paste thinly. Cut thin strips using the music stave cutter. Cut two strips to 7cm (2¾in). Attach one of the straps to the side of the bag.

5 Cut the end of the other strap to a point. Mark holes with a cocktail stick.

6 Stick the pointed end to the other strap and attach the other end to the bag.

7 Attach a short strap at the bottom of the bag and cut off the excess. Take another strap, cut the end to a point and mark holes with a cocktail stick.

8 Attach the pointed strap over the top of the bag, overlapping the bottom strap.

9 Cut some of the remaining bits of strip in half to make very thin strips. You need three.

10 Attach two very thin strips on the vertical bag strap and one around the handle strap.

11 Paint one on the bag and the other on the handle with edible gold paint to look like buckles. Indent the one on the bag with a cocktail stick.

Judith
This ladybird is struggling to count how many dots she has. Can you help her out?

LADYBIRD

Materials:

50g (1⅔oz) red modelling paste

60g (2⅛oz) black modelling paste

Small amount of white modelling paste

One red stripy chenille stick

One black chenille stick

Two white stamens

Red glitter

Butterfly wings

Cocktail stick

Tools:

Thin palette knife

Cocktail stick

Small circle cutters

Large icing tube

Small pair of scissors

Fine black fibre-tip pen

Sugar glue

Instructions:

1 Make a basic body in red as shown on page 20. Insert an 8cm (3¼in) cocktail stick and make two holes for the legs.

2 Roll a 20g (⅔oz) ball of black paste into a smooth ball for the head. Cut out a small white circle of modelling paste and glue it on to the front. Use a pointed tool to make two small holes for the eyes, one in the middle of the face for the nose, a small hole below that for the mouth and two holes on the top of the head for the antennae. Stick the stamens in the eye recesses and mark with the black pen. Roll a small ball of black paste for the nose and stick on.

3 Roll 3g (⅛oz) of red paste into a ball, cut in half and make two smaller balls. Cut the black chenille stick into two 5cm (2in) lengths, add glue to one end and attach a red ball. Lightly cover the ball with glue and dip it into the glitter. Shake off the excess. Push the other end into the top of the head with a little glue. Repeat for the second antenna.

4 Cut out 30 circles from black fondant (sugarpaste) using the small circle cutters. Use a little glue to attach them on to the body.

5 Cut a chenille stick in half and one piece in half again, to make two 7.5cm (3in) legs and one 15cm (6in) arm length.

6 Roll 10g of black paste into a ball and cut it in half to make two flat ovals for the shoes.

7 Make socks by rolling 6g (¼oz) of black paste into two small balls and placing one on top of each shoe with glue. Lightly glue each end of a 7.5cm (3in) chenille stick and

insert one end into the sock and shoe, and the other end into the body. Repeat.

8 For the hands, roll 6g (¼oz) of black paste into a ball. Cut it in half to make two balls. Add glue to each end of the 15cm (6in) chenille stick and attach one hand to each end. Bend the chenille stick around the back of the cocktail stick and glue it in place, bringing the arms and hands down. Bend the arms into shape when dry.

9 Attach the head to the body with a little sugar glue. Place the butterfly wings at the back and secure with glue or royal icing.

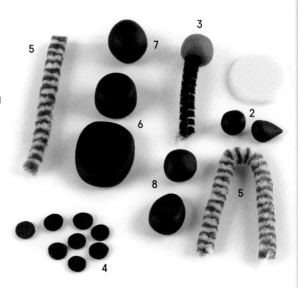

Lovely Lilies

These look great on their own or wired together with roses, freesias, orchids and foliage.

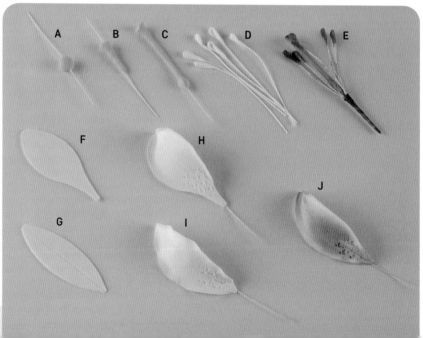

A   B   C   D   E

F   H

G   I   J

LILY

Materials:

- Mexican (flower/gum paste) in ivory and green
- Powdered food colour: yellow, light green, dark green, pink, burgundy
- Liquid food colour: burgundy

Tools:

- 26g wire: white (cut into quarter-lengths)
- Small veined lily plunger cutter: 60mm (2⅜in)
- Stem tape: green
- Paintbrushes: size 2/0 round, 12mm (½in) flat
- Dresden tool
- Ball tool

Instructions:

1 To make the pistil, roll a piece of green Mexican paste into a large pea-sized ball and push down on to a 26g wire (A).

2 Roll the paste with your fingers to elongate it along the wire and to shape it into a long slim bud shape, narrower at the base and wider at the top (B).

3 Flatten the end of the bud then divide the end into three, marking the divisions with a Dresden tool. Add a small ball of green paste at the base and pinch three equally spaced ridges vertically around it. Dust all over with light green petal dust and a little burgundy on the very top. Brush the top with glaze (C).

4 Gather together six ready-made lily stamens (D).

5 Colour them with yellow and burgundy petal dusts before taping the stamens around the base of the pistil with some stem tape.

6 Roll out a piece of Mexican paste to a thickness that will allow a 26g white wire to be inserted into it, then cut out and emboss three wide (F) and three narrow petals (G). Place them in a plastic food bag to keep them soft until you are ready to use them.

7 Carefully insert a wire into the base of each of the petals, pushing the wire three-quarters of the way up into the petal for support. Gently squash the paste on to the wire to secure.

8 Place the petals on to a foam pad and rub a ball tool around the edge of the petals to soften, thin and shape each one. With a pair of small fine-nosed scissors, snip into the paste at the base of the petals to create fine hairs. Bend the wire within the petals to a soft curve and dry over a gentle curve, such as a small rolling pin (H and I).

9 To colour, use the flat brush to add a little yellow and pale green powdered food colour at the bottom of each petal. Dust the whole of the centre of each petal with dark pink and burgundy, leaving a white outer edge. Paint the hairs and some tiny spots at the base of the petals with burgundy liquid colour using the size 2/0 paintbrush (J).

10 Once dry, use stem tape to secure the three wide petals together around the pistil before securing the three narrow petals immediately behind and in between the first three.

11 The flowers can be steamed to set the colour if required. Steam them over a pan of boiling water by just waving the flowers through the steam for a very short time. Holding them in the steam for too long will result in the flowers melting and falling off the wires. Leave to dry thoroughly.

Chocolate Sweetheart
The alternative has chocolate biscuit legs and arms, and cream-coloured icing. She could also be made by baking little cupcakes in the foil sweet cases. The icing swirls could be made with buttercream instead of royal icing.

CUPCAKE FAIRY

Materials:

10g (⅓oz) flesh-coloured
  fondant (sugarpaste)

White fondant (sugarpaste): 10g
  (⅓oz) for the body, 5g (⅙oz) for
  the shoes and hands

5g (⅙oz) pink modelling paste for
  the wings

Five candy sticks

Tiny amount of black
  fondant (sugarpaste)

Silver paper sweet case

Edible glitter

For the royal icing: 225g (8oz)
  icing/ confectioners' sugar, 1 egg
  white, half teaspoon glycerine

Tools:

Grease-free bowl

27mm (1in) heart cutter

Non-stick rolling pin

Small drinking straw

Thin palette knife

Plastic sandwich bag

Water brush

Dresden tool or cocktail stick

Piping bag and small star
  piping tube

Instructions:

1 To make the royal icing, beat the egg white in a grease-free bowl, add the icing sugar a little at a time and beat for a few minutes until it becomes a thick, creamy consistency and forms peaks. Mix in the glycerine.

2 For the wings, roll out pink modelling paste and cut out two hearts. Leave to dry for a few hours or overnight.

3 Make the legs from two candy sticks. For the shoes, make two pea-sized pieces of white fondant (sugarpaste) and shape each to a point. Attach the shoes.

4 Cut two holes on the bottom edge of the paper sweet case for the legs to be pushed in. Fill the case with a ball of fondant (sugarpaste) and push the legs in through the holes into the paste. Push in another candy stick vertically as support for the neck.

5 For the arms, cut candy sticks to 32mm (1¼in). Make two pea-sized pieces of white fondant (sugarpaste) and form each into a simple hand

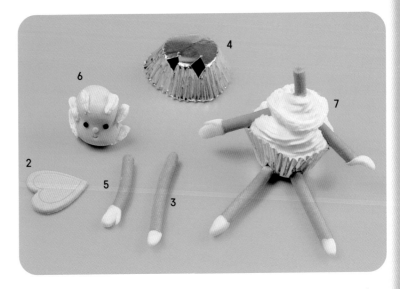

shape. Cut out tiny triangles to form thumbs. Attach to the arms.

6 Make the head following step 7, page 39.

7 Fill a piping bag with royal icing. Using a star piping tube, pipe a large swirl into the paper sweet case, up to the fairy's neck. Push the arms into the swirl and attach the wings while

the icing is still soft. For best results, allow this part to dry for a few hours before attaching the head.

8 Attach the head to the body with a little royal icing. For the hair, pipe a few strands towards the face, then pipe a spiral swirl to cover the head. Sprinkle with edible glitter while the icing is still soft.

Cock-a-Doodle-Doo!
Wakey wakey! It's time to start sugarcrafting this farmyard favourite! Use more earthy shades of fondant (sugarpaste) for the body, wings and tail, and lose the red comb and wattle to make a brood of hens to join your Rooster.

ROOSTER

Instructions:

1 For the tail feathers, roll some small pea-sized balls of the red, green and purple modelling paste. Form each of them into a thin cone approximately 2cm (¾in) long. Dampen the fat ends and press gently together with the tips fanning out. Curve the tips all in the same direction. Leave to dry.

2 To make the base, form a fat cube of the black paste. Make a hole in the centre of the cube using the dry candy stick and remove it.

3 Make six very thin, tiny cones of orange fondant (sugarpaste) for the feet. Stick them to the top of the base.

4 For the body, form a pointed oval of purple fondant (sugarpaste) 5cm (2in) long. Dampen the surface and lay a candy stick across the centre. Fold the purple fondant (sugarpaste) in half, bringing the points together and keeping the candy stick stuck inside, with each end sticking out of the paste. Curve the pointed end upwards for the tail.

5 For the head, shape the yellow fondant (sugarpaste) to a sausage 3cm (1¼in) long. Insert a dry candy stick lengthwise, almost to the end and then remove the stick. Pinch out the open end to widen it. Cut into the widened edge with scissors to make a zigzag edge. Dampen the inside edge of the paste and attach the head to the body over the stick. Make two small eyes from the black fondant (sugarpaste) and stick them on. Flatten a 1cm (⅜in) sausage of red fondant (sugarpaste), dampen along the top of the head, attach the paste and make indentations with the Dresden tool or a cocktail stick for the Rooster's comb.

6 Stick a very small orange cone on for the beak and cut across the middle with scissors to open it. Make two very small thin cones of red paste and attach them to the front of the face, just under the beak.

7 Dampen the candy stick and push the Rooster into the base, making sure it is vertical.

8 For the wings, take two pea-sized pieces of purple fondant (sugarpaste) and shape each into a cone, flatten, and mark on feathers with the Dresden tool or cocktail stick. Dampen them and attach them to the body, leaving the tips of the wings slightly apart. Dampen the base of the tail feathers and press them between the tips of the wings to attach them.

Materials:
White edible sugar candy stick

25g (just under 1oz) black modelling paste

Small amounts of red, green, orange, purple and black modelling paste

10g (⅓oz) purple fondant (sugarpaste)

5g (⅙oz) yellow fondant (sugarpaste)

Tools:
Sharp-pointed scissors

Dresden tool/cocktail stick

Edible sugar candy sticks

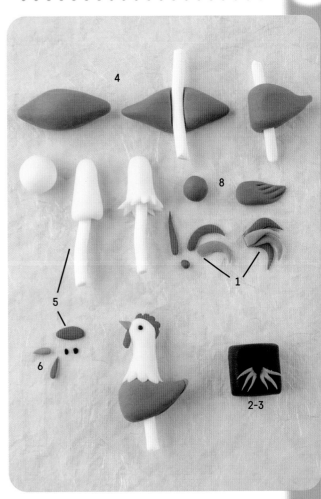

WICKED WITCH

Materials:

- 25g (1oz) black modelling paste
- Small amounts of pale green and orange fondant (sugarpaste)

Tools:

- Rolling pin
- 2.5cm (1in) and 1cm (½in) circle cutters
- Small, fine palette knife
- Food-grade kebab stick, barbecue stick or cake-pop stick 2cm (¾in) oval cutter
- Fine-mesh nylon sieve or tea strainer
- Dresden tool

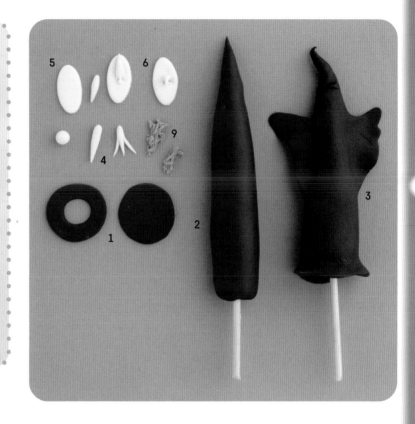

Instructions:

1 Roll out a small amount of the black modelling paste thinly. Cut out a 2.5cm (1in) circle and cut the centre out with the 1cm (½in) circle cutter.

2 Shape the rest of the black modelling paste into a 10cm (4in) long pointed carrot. Push the stick into the fat end as far as possible without it coming out at the top. Make sure that the 1cm (½in) cutter fits down the cone, as the black circle will form the rim of the hat. Mark a few lines on the hat part with a knife and shape it to look crooked.

3 Pinch the sides of the body out with your fingers to make simple, ragged sleeves. Pinch out the wide end with your fingers to make the base of the robe.

4 Make two tiny cones of pale green fondant (sugarpaste) for the hands. Cut into the pointed end to make at least three sharp-pointed fingers. Dampen the ends of the sleeves and attach the hands. Curve the sleeves over the ends of the hands.

5 Roll out the pale green fondant (sugarpaste) thinly. Cut a 2cm (¾in) oval.

6 Make a very tiny carrot of pale green fondant (sugarpaste) – half the length of the face. Stick it on the centre of the oval. Press the fat end with the Dresden tool to make nostrils. Curve the nose over to form a hooked nose.

7 Put the hat rim in place and dampen it slightly on the inner rim to secure it.

8 Dampen the back of the face and stick it under the rim of the hat. Use the wide end of the Dresden tool to push a mouth in, and the narrow end to mark the eyes. Make sure that you push the tool far enough into the black paste underneath to look dark.

9 Push a little orange paste through a fine-mesh nylon sieve or tea strainer to make fluff. Dampen around the face and attach the hair. Leave to dry overnight.

LEOPARD SHOE

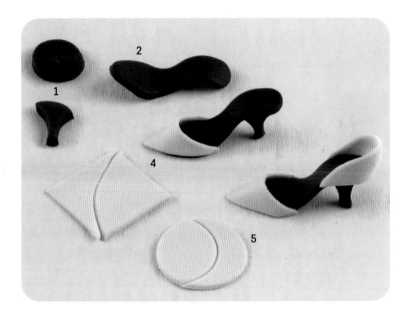

Materials:

- Mexican (flower/gum) paste in black and beige
- Dark brown and autumn leaf food colouring

Tools:

- Small non-stick rolling pin
- 4cm (1½in) shoe sole cutter
- 2.5cm (1in) and 1.5cm (⅝in) circle cutters
- 2.5cm (1in) square cutter
- Dowel
- Small fine palette knife
- Cutting wheel
- Dresden tool
- Dogbone/ball tool
- Small sharp pointed scissors
- Waterbrush/small paintbrush and water
- Small fine paintbrush

Instructions:

1 Roll out the black paste to a thickness of 2mm (⅒in). Cut out a 1.5cm (⅝in) circle. Use the 2.5cm (1in) circle cutter to cut across the middle to form the back curve of the heel. Cut again using the 1.5cm (⅝in) circle cutter to form the front curve of the heel. Allow the heel to dry for a few minutes, turning it over occasionally.

2 Roll out the black paste to a thickness of 1mm (⅟₂₀in). Cut out the 4cm (1½in) sole. Rest the heel end over a dowel for a few minutes to create the high-heeled look, until the sole feels leathery.

3 Dampen the top curve of the wheel and attach under the sole. Lay the shoe on its side and cut a tiny piece off the point of the heel to enable it to stand straight. Stand the shoe up and allow to dry for at least 30 minutes.

4 Roll out the beige paste thinly. Allow to dry slightly on each side until the paste feels leathery. Cut out a 2.5cm (1in) square and a 2.5cm (1in) circle. Use the cutting wheel to cut across the square diagonally with a slight curve. Dampen the straight edges underneath and stick them to the sides of the sole to make the toe piece of the shoe.

5 Using the 2.5cm (1in) circle cutter, cut the beige circle to make a crescent moon shape for the shoe back. Cup the inside with the dogbone/ball tool. Dampen the inside curve underneath and attach it to the back of the sole.

6 To create the leopard spots, paint tiny, roughly circular outlines of dark brown all over the beige parts, and then fill the outlines with autumn leaf colouring. Allow to dry.

SHEEPDOG

Materials:

30g (1oz) pink modelling paste

25g (just under 1oz) white modelling paste

20g (⅔oz) white fondant (sugarpaste)

Small amount of grey fondant (sugarpaste)

Edible candy sticks

Edible black sugar pearls

Tools:

Dresden tool

Water brush

Thin palette knife

Cutting wheel

Stitching wheel

Small non-stick rolling pin

Plastic food bag/airtight box

Instructions:

1 Roll out pink modelling paste thickly. Cut a blanket approximately 8 x 6cm (3⅛ x 2⅜in). Mark with the stitching wheel.

2 Shape 15g (½oz) white modelling paste to a 6cm (2⅜in) sausage for the body. At one end, pinch and shape a small tail. At the other end, press and pinch to widen it slightly. Dampen the widened part and wrap it around the top of two 6cm (2⅜in) edible candy sticks. Lift the whole body and legs on to the blanket. Push the legs vertically into the blanket, place the body and tail in a sitting position and dampen to attach the dog.

3 Make a 5g (⅙oz) long pear shape of white modelling paste for the head. Gently pinch down the sides of the narrow end to form the muzzle. Mark indentations for the eyes and nose using the Dresden tool and insert edible black sugar pearls.

4 Make a tiny cone of pink modelling paste for the tongue, flatten it slightly, dampen and attach it so it hangs out of the mouth. Make a tiny cone of white paste for the bottom

jaw and stick it in with the rounded end under the nose. Dampen the top of the neck and push the head gently into place. Allow to dry for a couple of hours or overnight.

5 Shape lots of tiny 1–2cm (⅜–¾in) sausages of white fondant (sugarpaste) and a few grey ones for fur. Keep them in a plastic food bag or airtight box to keep them soft. Dampen the candy stick legs and attach two or three tiny sausages at a time, starting at the paws and draping over the blanket. Use the Dresden tool or knife to mark long fur, thinning it where it lies over the blanket. Continue up the legs, overlapping the paste, and making it look like long fur up to the neck. The fur should cover the candy sticks. Dampen the tail and add more long fur to drape over the blanket. Continue up the body, making patches of grey and blending in each time. On the head, start in the middle of the head and nose, so that the fur hangs down.

6 Stick a few strands together and attach to the sides of the head, pointing upwards, and then let the fur bend down sideways. Add more strands where needed.

MONKEY

Instructions:

1 Divide the brown fondant (sugarpaste), taking about 35g (1¼oz) to make an egg shape for the body. A hardened candy stick can be pushed right into the body, leaving a small piece at the top to help support the head.

2 Make a thin sausage of brown fondant (sugarpaste) for the tail. Coil up the end and attach to the bottom of the body.

3 Take a pea-sized piece of brown fondant (sugarpaste) for the ears, and press a smaller ball of peach on top. Cut in half across the top. Divide the rest of the brown paste into five equal balls.

4 Make four of the brown balls into long sausages for the legs and arms. Bend each in the middle for the knees and elbow.

5 Make four hands from small peach-coloured cones. Flatten slightly, and cut one long thumb and four fingers on each. Make two left- and two right-handed.

6 Attach the legs and arms to the body. Stick on the hands.

7 Take the fifth brown ball for the head and attach it to the body. Position the arms as shown.

8 Dampen the cut edge of the ears and attach to the side of the head.

9 For the face, cut out a heart shape in peach fondant (sugarpaste), using the heart cutter. Stick a small oval of peach at the bottom of the heart. Mark a wide mouth with a knife. Mark nostrils with a cocktail stick.

10 Stick on eyes made from two tiny balls of black fondant (sugarpaste) and attach the face to the head.

Materials:

100g (3½oz) brown or chocolate fondant (sugarpaste)

20g (⅔oz) peach fondant (sugarpaste)

Small amount of black fondant (sugarpaste)

Candy stick

Tools:

Cocktail stick

Sharp pointed scissors

Thin palette knife

Heart cutter, 2.5cm (1in)

231

Hot Lips
These lippy sugar bags can be made with the lips open or tightly zipped. Make them to adorn a cake for a bag lover with a sense of humour as well as a sense of style.

RED LIPS

Materials:

Mexican (flower/gum) paste
  in red
Edible silver paint
Tiny silver-coloured sugar balls
Piping gel

Tools:

Small, non-stick rolling pin
Dresden tool
Cutting wheel
Large stitching wheel
Fine paintbrush
Ruler

Instructions:

1 Roll two sausages of paste approximately 6cm x 5mm (2⅜ x ¼in).

2 Pinch the ends together. Make the top lip shape by pushing in the middle with a Dresden tool.

3 Roll the paste thinly. Allow to dry slightly on the surface.

4 Lay the lip shape on top of the paste. Cut closely around the shape for one piece and about 1cm (⅜in) larger for the second.

5 Attach the lip shape on top of the smaller mouth.

6 Use the large stitching wheel to mark two stitching lines along the middle of the larger mouth shape. If the mouth is to be unzipped, cut between the stitching lines.

7 Dampen the back of the paste and lay it over the lip shape. Shape the paste over and pinch the pointed ends. Mark gentle creases in the lips with the Dresden tool.

8 Brush over the surface with piping gel and a fine paintbrush. Attach silver-coloured sugar balls at one end of the zip.

9 Paint the zip with edible silver paint and a fine paintbrush. Handle the bag carefully as it will stay tacky.

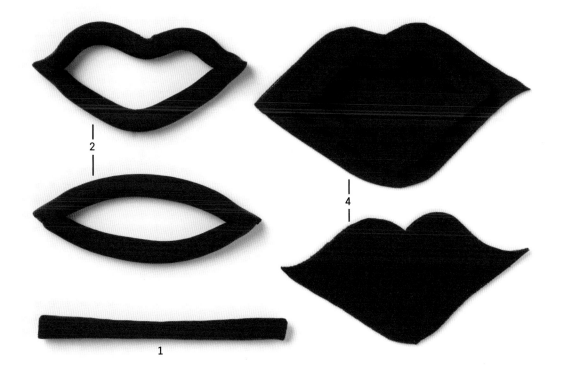

This is Sure to Take Off
Try using different brightly-coloured fondant (sugarpaste) and coloured pearl powders; such as blue fondant (sugarpaste) with lilac pearl powder, red fondant (sugarpaste) with gold powder or green fondant (sugarpaste) with pink pearl powder. The shimmer really lifts your sugar creations.

HUMMINGBIRD

Materials:

5g (⅙oz) purple fondant (sugarpaste)

Small amount of black fondant (sugarpaste)

Edible wafer paper

Edible powder colour: deep pink

Edible powder pearl colour: frosty holly

Purple food colour felt-tip pen

Tools:

Sharp-pointed scissors

Dusting brush

Sharp knife

No. 2 piping tube

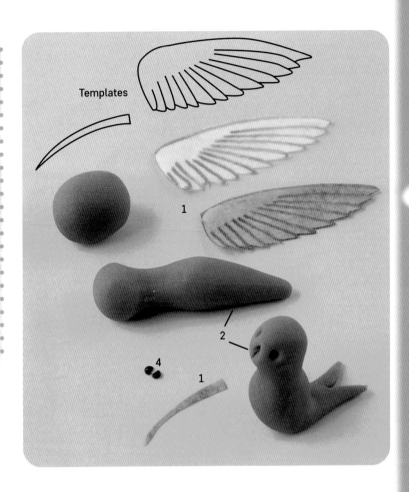

Templates

Instructions:

1 On edible wafer paper, draw two wings and a beak with the food colour felt-tip pen, using the templates provided. Carefully cut them out. Turn the wafer paper wings over and draw the wings on the other side. Brush the bird's beak and wings with the dry edible powder colour in deep pink.

2 For the body, shape the purple fondant (sugarpaste) to a 5cm (2in) long cone. Roll the wide end between your two fingers to form the neck, and cut out a V-shape for the tail. Bend the body to stand it up. With sharp-pointed scissors, mark two short vertical lines into the back for the wings and a short vertical line for the beak. Mark on two holes for the eye sockets using the no. 2 piping tube.

3 Brush edible powder pearl colour in frosty holly over the body.

4 Make two tiny eyes from black fondant (sugarpaste), dampen the eye sockets and stick them on.

5 Very lightly dampen the scissor-marks and insert the beak and the wings.

ARACHNOPHOBIA

Materials:

12.5g (⁷⁄₁₆oz) black
    modelling paste

10g (³⁄₈oz) red modelling paste

Black edible food colour powder

Edible black sugar pearls

Tools:

Dresden tool

Dusting brush

Small, fine palette knife

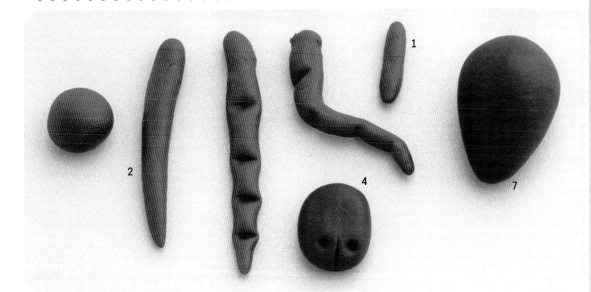

Instructions:

1 For the jaws, shape two very small, pea-sized pieces of red modelling paste into 2cm (³⁄₄in) sausages. Press in three indentations using the Dresden tool down the length of each sausage without cutting through.

2 Make eight large, pea-sized pieces of red modelling paste, all the same size, for the legs. Roll each leg into a thin, pointed 5cm (2in) carrot shape. Press in four indentations using the Dresden tool down the length of each one without cutting through. Curve each leg and bend out each foot. Press the rounded end gently to flatten it slightly.

3 Brush gently across each joint of the legs and the jaws with black edible food colour powder.

4 For the head, shape 2.5g (¹⁄₈oz) of black modelling paste into a ball. Make two holes for the eyes, dampen the eye sockets and attach the black sugar pearls. Mark hairs along the head with the knife .

5 Attach the jaws at the front of the head, under the eyes.

6 Dampen each leg at the flattened end and attach four down each side of the body, making sure the legs are curved with the feet pointing out.

7 Shape 10g (³⁄₈oz) of black modelling paste into an egg shape to make the abdomen. Mark hairs along the abdomen with the knife. Dampen the narrow end and attach it to the back of the head.

MEN'S SLIPPERS

Materials:

Mexican (flower/gum) paste in brown

Dark green edible powder food colour

Tools:

Small non-stick rolling pin

3cm (1¼in) oval cutter

2.5cm (1in) circle cutter

Small fine palette knife

Music stave cutter

Waterbrush or small paintbrush and water

Design wheel

Dusting brush

Instructions:

1 Roll out the paste to a thickness of 2mm (¹⁄₁₀in). Cut out a 3cm (1¼in) oval to make the sole of the slipper.

2 Roll out the paste thinly. Cut out a 2.5cm (1in) circle.

3 Emboss lines on the circle using the music stave cutter.

4 Use the dusting brush to colour the raised surface with dark green edible powder food colour. The embossed lines will stay brown if you only use a small amount of colour.

5 Mark stitches around half of the circle using the design wheel. Dampen around the side edge of the sole. Attach the front of the slipper from the toe end.

If you would like more information about sugarcraft, try the following books, all published by Search Press:

Cake Decorating for Beginners

Fun Figures by Lorraine McKay

Airbrushing on Cakes by Cassie Brown